CAREERS
PHOTOG

David Higgs

Second Edition

KOGAN PAGE
CAREERS
SERIES

First published in 1983 by Kogan Page Ltd
120 Pentonville Road, London N1 9JN
Second edition 1988

British Library Cataloguing in Publication Data

Higgs, David *1952-*
Careers in photography. - 2nd ed.
1. Photography - Vocational guidance -
Great Britain
I. Title
770'.23'2 TR154

ISBN 1-85091-386-2

Typeset by DP Photosetting, Aylesbury, Bucks
Printed and bound in Great Britain
by Richard Clay, The Chaucer Press, Bungay

Contents

Introduction

This book looks at the whole range of career opportunities associated with still photography. This means not only jobs involved with taking photographs, but also those in supporting and allied professions such as photographic laboratories and aspects of the retail trade.

As well as indicating what types of training and qualifications are required in the different career areas, some of the advantages and disadvantages of each are indicated. Individual career case studies have been included in certain sections of the book to give the reader at first hand an insight into the different jobs available.

In the present economic climate, it is often very difficult to find employment, let alone assess the long-term prospects of any particular career. However, where possible I have tried to give an indication of relative job security.

Although in principle all career areas offer equal opportunities to both men and women, in practice there is disparity, at least in terms of those who could be called 'successful'. Where relevant, I have tried to point out those factors which may weigh against a woman competing against a man for a particular job.[1] This is not meant to dissuade, but to equip a girl to cope with the job situation or the possible 'sticky' interview question. One good example is that of physical strength, because in some situations there may be no other alternative than having to carry a lot of heavy equipment and being able to move very fast indeed! There are also situations where a woman may have distinct advantages over a man. In the final analysis it is competence and determination that count.

It should also be emphasised that you should not restrict yourself to one specific area, but try to look at the employment

---

[1] Although 'he' is used throughout this book, it is for convenience only, and not meant to suggest that all photographers are men.

situation as a whole. Anyone attempting to find a career at the present time, should at least be aware that too much specialisation at an early stage may lead into a career 'blind alley', with few alternatives when circumstances change for the worse or require flexibility of expertise.

To some extent the organisation of this book into separate sections covering different areas of photographic specialisation is artificial. Indeed, too much specialisation could be very short-sighted of a photographer from the business point of view. This is especially so in the present economic climate, where the number of commissions and assignments available are few. The freelance and general purpose photographer in particular needs considerable versatility in order to attract a variety of different jobs. This is to generate a cash flow which will maintain the viability of his business. These distinctions have been made simply to clarify the situation, and for the ease of the reader who is interested in a particular field of photography.

It should be emphasised that to get a balanced view of the employment situation as a whole, and to avoid the pitfall of becoming too specialised at an early stage of your career, it is recommended that you should look at all the different sections to better appreciate the relationship between your area of interest and the industry as a whole. To facilitate this, Chapter 1, 'The World of Professional Photography', tries to give a general overview of the profession and the way in which photographers, the 'support' industries and society interrelate.

The final chapters of the book are a compendium of training courses and establishments. Full-time, part-time, evening and correspondence courses are listed. The last section quotes a number of addresses which may be useful to anyone requiring further guidance or information. Journals and publications in which job advertisements most often appear, as well as suggested further reading and references, are also included.

Part 1

Chapter 1

The World of Professional Photography

Introduction

The need for photography and its products has now become totally inseparable from western society. What began only 150 years ago as a scientific novelty has come to dominate most aspects of life.

In this modern information-hungry world photography and its associated industries have come to play a crucial part. Any industry will only continue to grow so long as there is a demand for its products. In this respect, photography occupies a privileged position but also as a result, competition, especially among photographers, is extremely intense.

Anyone seeking a career in photography should remember that the job of photographer is just a small part of a whole spectrum of related professions. However, much of this spectrum requires a blend of both artistic and technical abilities. It is this aspect of photography which makes it such a unique and exciting area in which to start a career.

The requirement for a blend of talents means that there is scope for the employment of people with a wide variety of temperaments and abilities. It should be pointed out that not everyone can be a photographer; for every job available in this field there are probably ten on offer in the supporting industries. Once again, it is important to try to keep your options as open as possible. Few people actually go straight into work as a photographer; it is more usual to take an indirect route by first becoming an assistant in a laboratory or studio.

The photographic industry exists to supply society's constant need for photographic material. The last link in the supply chain is usually the photographer, of whom there are two types, the amateur and the professional. Almost certainly the greatest market for equipment, materials and service is created by the amateur photographer. However, the photographs which have the most impact on our daily lives are taken by professional photographers. For these reasons, the greatest opportunities for employment lie in those industries connected with the amateur market, while the greatest prestige and competition is for jobs involved with the professional field. This distinction between the two markets has been made to emphasise the wide diversity of employment possible within the industry. It also has the purpose of trying to prevent the prospective employee from being dazzled by the glamour of the professional world, by making him aware of the great range of jobs available in industries supplying the needs of the amateur. However, it is also true to say that to some extent there is considerable overlap between the two supporting industries, and this does allow for flexibility of employment prospects and advancement.

How Important is Photography Today?

Photography has revolutionised education. The photographic image has an advantage over the written word, in that it does not need to be translated for use in another country or society. It is by and large an international means of communication. Its application in medicine, such as X-rays, for research, investigation and documentation, is immense. The news media and all forms of published information rely heavily on the photographic image. The detection and investigation of crime involves the use of simple photographic techniques and also highly sophisticated ones, where photographs are taken with special cameras, hidden details are revealed using ultra-violet light photography, and so on. The storage and retrieval of information has been made considerably more convenient, and involves the use of far less space now that the technique of microfilming is so widely used.

The purchase of products, which once would have been considered beyond the reach of most people's finances, has been made possible by the use of photography in mass advertising. This has caused manufacturers and retailers to sell their wares at lower prices. There is also a huge demand for social photography - the recording of all the important events in people's lives which fill albums in virtually every home in the western world.

Employment Opportunities

As mentioned, for every photographer there is a host of others in the supporting industries. All the manufacturers of film, paper, chemicals, cameras, lenses and other equipment employ vast numbers of chemists, engineers and scientists whose job it is to develop, research and improve products available to the amateur and professional alike. Besides this is the whole public relations, advertising and marketing machinery involved in the sale of these products. The retailers, shop managers and assistants should be reasonably competent and knowledgeable photographers who can give reliable information and advice to the customer.

All photographic equipment needs periodic servicing if it is to give accurate and reliable service, and of course equipment sometimes needs to be repaired. Photographic laboratories should be staffed with trained technicians to operate processing and printing machines. In certain fields, considerable artistic flair may be required, especially in printing and retouching. Here an individual's skill and ability to interpret the final effect that the photographer was trying to achieve is paramount.

A photographic studio requires not only photographers, but assistants, make-up artists, secretaries and tea-boys. The latter occupation has been the starting point for a large number of now highly successful photographers.

Lastly, we come to the institutional and training aspect of the industry. There are professional associations, unions and training establishments for the different sectors of the industry. These will be dealt with in more detail in the appropriate section of the book. However, each of these also has to be staffed or represented by committed and experienced individuals, who are concerned to see a responsible development of their profession.

Qualities Required

So far we have outlined the requirement for a blend of artistic and scientific skills, the latter often being the result of careful training and education, but there is also a need for individuals with social skills. For instance, the general practice photographer, who is called to record weddings and other events, must be a person who is at ease with strangers and who can put others at ease. This applies at many levels of the industry where one has to deal with children, customers and clients.

The Future

In an age where employment is threatened by mechanisation and the silicon chip, it is at least some comfort to know that the creative photographer is highly unlikely to ever be replaced by a machine. However, these innovations will continue to have increasing impact on the developing, printing and manufacturing side of the profession. On the other hand, as a result of the increase in sophistication, miniaturisation and cheapness of production of photographic equipment and materials, more and more people are finding photography an accessible and affordable hobby. The result is more opportunities for employment.

It should be clear by now just how complex this industry has become. This also means that it does offer considerable scope for employment. But it should not be forgotten that a very special mix of social, artistic and considerable scientific skill is required in most of its areas. The particular combination of these skills and your determination to succeed in this fiercely competitive occupation, will largely determine which branch of the profession you enter.

Chapter 2

Commercial Photography

Advertising and Publicity

This type of work is highly specialised, demanding and competitive in the extreme. Although this work can fall into the province of the general practice and freelance photographer, the mainstream and most lucrative aspects of this work will be beyond their resources. Generally, such assignments go to highly esteemed photographers, who have considerable experience in a particular field, and who have access to well equipped studio facilities. Usually, the work is assigned through an advertising agency; less often, the photographer will be approached directly by the client.

Many photographers are attracted by the world of advertising because it can yield extremely large fees. Ambitious individuals, who visualise their bank accounts bulging at the seams, often fall back to earth with a tremendous bump, however, when they realise how difficult it is to become established.

Advertising is by nature a competitive business, and manufacturers and their advertising agents are always on the look-out for photographers who can produce pictures which are original and stunning. They aim to attract the consumer's attention, to show how desirable or superior their product is in comparison to everyone else's. The photographer must fulfil these requirements, and he needs to be imaginative and creative as well as having a high degree of technical knowledge.

The subjects of advertising photography can vary enormously from items of food to exotic holidays. The pictures may also be used in a variety of media, such as brochures, posters or advertisements in national publications. The photographer must know not only how to shoot the product to best advantage but also choose an approach which is best suited to the media for which the photograph is intended.

For the purpose of a large advertising campaign, the client usually consults an advertising agency. Together they decide on an image and approach which will best sell the product, and the media that will best project the advertisement to the intended market. If the advertisement requires a photograph, the art director creates a design to suggest what the finished advertisement will look like. Space is allowed for any copy (words), and a detailed drawing used to indicate how the desired photograph will appear. If the client approves the layout, it is only at this stage that a photographer may be approached, taking into account the budget available for photography. Sometimes several photographers may be approached and invited to submit tenders for the work. In this case, they may be expected to submit their own ideas on how the final photograph will appear. The photographer who obtains the job is not necessarily the cheapest, but the one with the most original and striking idea. The agency must also be convinced that the photographer is capable of carrying out his idea.

The photographer often has to work exactly to the art director's brief for the finished photograph. He may either be given a sketch or a written description. Very often the art director will be at the shoot to ensure that the photographic results are exactly as intended. Sometimes the photographer is expected to interpret the intentions of the art director, or to come up with a twist or effect which will make a stunning photograph. It is this latter ability which makes the difference between the top flight of advertising photographers who have a steady stream of work, and those who struggle to pick up what is left.

Not only has the photographer to work under the constant pressure of thinking up new ideas, but also there is often little time to complete each job. He must be versatile, and able to work equally well whether in the studio or on location. He may be expected to find suitable props to be used for a particular photograph. He must also have the technical 'know how' to be able to use a wide variety of cameras, lenses and lighting equipment. With this knowledge, he can satisfactorily photograph a large studio set-up, such as a mock-up of a room; and small items, for example a pack-shot (a close-up of a product) or still-life.

Case Study

Steven, an *advertising photographer*, has been building up his own studio over the last few years.

At the age of eight, I was given a box camera by my parents and started taking black and white photographs. By the time I reached secondary school, I had read a great many books on photography, and had begun developing and printing my own pictures in the bathroom at home.

I went to a college of art to take a three-year course in photography consisting of practical work, theory and business studies.

After completing my course successfully, I became a photographic assistant at a small photographic studio. The duties of an assistant involve quite a lot of physical work – moving large pieces of equipment about, loading film, processing of black and white material and overall responsibility for seeing that the studio and its equipment are kept in good working order.

All my experience was gained by watching the photographer, whom I assisted. I worked on different jobs with different lighting set-ups, and saw how he handled different clients and art directors.

After several years as an assistant, I made the break from the studio to work on my own within advertising. This required a portfolio of my own work which I could show to advertising agencies. I took the photographs for the portfolio while I was an assistant, in my own time. I also needed a studio to work from, and a great deal of equipment.

I then moved to share a studio with another photographer in London. I started working very steadily, and purchased small items of equipment as I went along. As commissions became more complicated, I had to hire additional equipment. Finally, I had to raise a large loan from my bank and buy the equipment needed.

As the volume of work increased I had to move to my own studio to have sufficient space to work in.

This was very expensive, and once again I had to ask my bank for a large amount of money.

I feel I must stress the precarious nature of the profession, and the difficulties encountered in obtaining and maintaining a consistent level of work. Advertising photography, by its very nature, is subject to constant fluctuations, and obtaining a share of the available work is not easy in such a highly competitive profession. Difficulty in obtaining work is most noticeable in your earlier years. Before you have established a reputation, advertising agencies are very reluctant to commit large sums of a client's money in commissioning a relatively untried photographer.

I now work both in the studio and on location for major advertising agencies. I have produced beer posters, worked on car campaigns and many other subjects that appear in magazines and on poster sites.

Fashion

The fashion photographer needs to have the same technical expertise and facilities as the general advertising photographer. Very often, a photographic studio is involved with both types of work. However, it is often an area where photographers specialise almost exclusively. Fashion photography is all about style and showing clothing, shoes, hats, stockings, underwear and make-up to the best possible advantage. To be successful in this area, the photographer needs to take pictures that are both distinctive, and portray the kind of image and style which the art director wishes to communicate. The photographer has to be able to portray the human form and garments in a way which makes them highly desirable.

Because he spends much of his time working with models, it is vital that he has the right temperament and personality. He must be able to coax and encourage the model to show the garment off in the most attractive way possible, while still retaining a pleasant and relaxed atmosphere. Often this has to be done while working against the clock!

The photographer may have to employ or hire make-up artists and hair stylists as well as other staff. He may have to choose his own models and book them. He must, therefore, be a good organiser. If he forgets one important item it may mean that the shoot is cancelled, causing loss of reputation and money, or postponed, which may cause problems due to clashes with other jobs which are already booked. He must be equally adept at working in a controlled studio situation or in a more unpredictable location situation.

Whether one works as a general advertising or fashion photographer, job security is limited. If you have a distinctive style it may become unfashionable. Unless you can develop another style quickly, and one which is also attractive, you may find that customers become fewer. If you make a mistake over a job, or the art director or client feels your work has not come up to expectations, you may find that you are not used again. The photographer must be sufficiently versatile, technically competent and creative to be able to adjust to new fashions, styles and economic situations if he is to survive.

Starting in Advertising and Fashion Photography

Entry to professions in both advertising and fashion photography is usually gained by beginning as a messenger or as a general assistant. You must be prepared for the fact that you may be, sometimes for several years, the 'lowest form of life' in the studio. Much of your time may be spent making tea, sweeping floors, running messages and answering the telephone. Eventually as your experience increases, you may begin to assist in the setting up of studio lighting, loading cameras, booking models and so on. By this stage, you may be regarded as a photographer's assistant. However, it may still be some time before you are entrusted to take any photographs for the less important jobs.

Fashion photographers actually rarely employ untrained assistants. For this reason, competition for these posts, which are very few, is very fierce. London is one of the few places where there is a market for freelance photographic assistants, but you can expect the competition to be severe. Sooner or later, once you have begun to do some photographic work yourself, you must begin to compile a 'book' or portfolio of your photography. Your portfolio should reflect the best of your work, and accurately portray your range of technical and creative expertise. You must then be prepared to spend a lot of time going from one advertising agency's art buyer to the next, selling yourself and your work. It can be lonely, exhausting and dispiriting, and it may take several years before you achieve a real 'break'. The only consolation is that this is the way that nearly every successful commercial photographer has begun his career.

Salary

Nearly all photographers involved in advertising and fashion are paid according to a day rate. This is a rate which is agreed between the photographer and his client or agent. It can vary between £200 and £1,000 per day, and reflects the professional standing of the individual concerned. If you are not an established name you may have to work for much less and, in general, rates for this type of work are lower outside London. Obviously you are only paid for those days you work.

Case Study

Tom, a *fashion photographer*, originally wanted to be a cinematographer, and went to film school. During his third and final year, he began to feel that the 'system' of finding work in films was too slow and unsatisfactory. He felt he would have a better chance of starting his own projects if he moved towards still photography.

At that time, he was not interested in fashion or advertising photography as a career. So instead of beginning by assisting a studio photographer, he spent two years doing 'his own thing' - shooting colour essays, and subsidising his income by doing gardening and dish washing jobs.

After enduring 'the starving artist' syndrome for some time, he suffered a blow which would have finished many people. While in America his entire portfolio was lost. At this stage *Life* had been considering the publication of one of his essays.

He returned to the UK wondering if the 'starving' had all been worthwhile. He began to build up a new portfolio and approached one or two advertising agencies. At this stage, his portfolio comprised mostly picture essays and landscapes, very little was 'commercial' photography.

An art buyer at one of the agencies liked some of his work, and introduced him to a studio manager who was looking for extra photographers to share a studio complex. They were looking for someone young with fresh ideas to do fashion photography. This was the start of his commercial career.

He learnt mostly by trial and error, and had to accept that to survive he had to do things that some 'pure' photographers, including himself in the early days, would have regarded as sacrilege.

Over the next 12 years, Tom gradually developed the business and finally achieved his own studio, but the first seven years were a real financial struggle.

> There are many misconceptions about the earnings and lifestyle of fashion photographers. During those early years, I certainly didn't have a flashy car or a 'groovy King's Road pad'.
>
> Since then I have even had to sacrifice doing some of the work which I enjoyed in order to make a secure living. I finally phased out still lifes a few years ago. I was quite sad about this, because I did enjoy the contrast of one day doing fashion and the next photographing a drinks slot. But to be successful in this business, it is really important to be known for something that you specialise in. So now it's 90 per cent people and, of them, 90 per cent are women in some context or other.
>
> Of my working time now, a large part is spent organising and running the business. A surprisingly small amount of my time is actually spent 'on the camera'.

I often find it amusing, but sometimes irritating, that during a day's beauty shoot everyone else, including hairdresser, make-up artist, stylist and others, have more of the model's time than the photographer! On average I am allowed 20–30 minutes per shot.

To compensate for this imbalance, I try to spend some time working on personal projects as far removed from advertising photography as possible.

I am quite sure that the loss of my portfolio in America represented a crucial point in my career, and was largely responsible for my move towards commercial photography. I think, like in so many careers, timing is a most crucial factor. The right face in the right place at the right time.

Mail Order

Mail order photography is really a branch of advertising work. Unlike a decade or more ago, very few mail order companies now run their own studios. The majority of work is undertaken by established professional freelance photographers with experience in the particular field. The Association of Master Photographers estimated that in 1986 there were fewer than 3,000 photographers employed full-time by mail order companies.

Salary

As for advertising and fashion photography.

Industrial

Industry employs a considerable number of photographers. These can either be 'in-plant' or freelance. Generally, the freelance is a specialist who is contracted in to do work which is considered to be outside the scope of expertise of the in-plant man. Freelance industrial photography may have a little more glamour but a less regular salary.

Often the industry's own photographer may be expected to do a wide variety of jobs by himself. If the industry is very large he may be one of several photographers, possibly with the back-up of a darkroom and technical staff. In a small industry, he may operate very much like a general practice photographer. He must be able to get on well with a variety of people – for example the factory staff, whose cooperation may be vital – and work in a variety of situations – for example covering the firm's sports day, or the boss's retirement party. He may be expected to do a lot of general publicity, and produce illustrations for brochures, catalogues and instruction manuals.

In a highly technical industry, photography may be used as part of quality control and the detection of faults in manufactured goods. This may be in the form of high speed and close-up photography.

Some aspects of industrial photography allow considerable scope for individual creativity. One must have the ability to make a dreary factory site look exciting and interesting. If you take the time to look at some really good examples of a skilled photographer's work, you will be amazed at how a comparatively uninteresting machine or component has been portrayed as a work of art.

Physical strength is required to carry heavy equipment from one end of a factory to another. You may be required to work outside in severe and hostile weather conditions. You don't need much imagination to visualise the conditions you might encounter on an oil rig or a dam building operation.

Where much of the photography is highly technical a formal course of training is required. Generally you begin as a trainee photographer or technician, and progress through junior and senior posts to chief photographer or chief audio-visual technician. Applicants for advertised posts are preferred to have college diplomas. However, if you have no photographic qualifications, generally school-leavers are more likely to get a job than an older applicant. Those unable to secure a trainee opening are best advised to get some all-round or technical experience elsewhere, with a view to entry later on at a higher level.

Photographic jobs in industry are usually very secure, one rarely has to work under pressure, and there are often many fringe benefits. For this reason, such posts are very popular, and because there are always many more applicants wanting these jobs than there are opportunities, competition is very fierce. Job vacancies are advertised in the trade press or through photographic employment agencies.

Industry often employs a large number of scientific photographers. This field is dealt with more fully in the next chapter.

Salary

This is a very diverse industry, and it is not possible to indicate wage levels. Salary very much depends on the size of the establishment, and the importance of the photographic department within the industry. You are best advised to make specific enquiries to those companies which you think would be the most interesting to work for.

General Practice

About half of all professional photographers are employed in what is called general practice. This is the photographer whom you find on the high street in your town. They are mostly involved in social photography, for example, photographing weddings, christenings and graduations. Many photographers involved in general practice have a shop attached to their studio. Studio work is normally in the form of portraiture, although businesses which have a more commercial orientation may do some advertising work for local companies and advertising agencies. Since nearly all their work involves working closely with young people, sometimes in a small community, a warm, friendly personality is a must.

The nature of one's business often depends on the location. If you are situated in a highly industrialised area, your work may involve a lot of industrial type photography. You may also be expected to take a lot of public relations photographs of work forces, managers and directors for local business publications and newspapers.

If the business is in a thriving town, you may find yourself taking portraits in the morning, and photographs at a dress rehearsal at the local theatre in the afternoon. You may also be expected to undertake some press photography for the local newspaper. For example, you may be asked to cover the opening of a new shopping centre, football matches and other sporting events.

Employment opportunities and the chances of advancement depend very much on the size of the practice. Many are small family concerns, where there will be little chance of obtaining any more than basic 'shop assistant' experience. Large firms, which are involved in developing and processing, may have a variety of trainee positions available with the possibility of moving on to photographer's assistant.

Experience at the technical level, printing and processing may be useful if you decide to move into the laboratory side of the trade. Certainly to run your own business successfully in the future you will need adaptability, initiative and physical fitness. You must also be prepared to go out and find a lot of your own business. You must, therefore, have the confidence to be able to sell yourself and be able to deal with a variety of people. You will need the ability to deal with the occasional irate customer and be cool and soothing, to cope with an over-energetic child whose mother wants a portrait, and then drive over to a nearby factory to take some shots of a busy and impatient businessman - all without getting flustered.

Starting a Career

Some of the larger general practices have openings for assistants or trainees. This may be one way of achieving some experience. Photographers also move into this field after working in other commercial and press fields. If you want to start work straight away as a photographer experience is essential. A college training course may be useful, and certainly will give you extra career flexibility. Many general practices also have their own developing and processing laboratories which may provide another opening for someone hoping to gain experience.

Vacancies for social and wedding photographers are advertised in the trade press and by photographic employment agencies. The same applies also to industrial vacancies.

Salary

Salary levels vary considerably and depend on age, skill and experience. Trainee salaries are especially variable and generally low. Many of the advertisements for social and wedding photographers with some experience quote starting salaries of about £4,500 per annum. The low salary reflects the fact that the number of young photographers wanting to get a foothold in the industry greatly exceeds the opportunities and openings.

Case Study

John is a partner and managing director of a *provincial photographic agency*. He manages a comprehensive practice as well as doing some commercial work.

> I entered photography quite by accident. I applied along with 50 others for the job of darkroom boy on the local morning and evening newspaper in my home town. I had in fact been offered a number of other jobs but this one seemed to mean more exciting work, so I accepted.
>
> After a couple of years spent making tea, fetching and carrying, as well as watching the professional photographers at work, I was allowed to 'tag along' with them on all the sorts of jobs press

photographers undertake. I felt I might make a nuisance of myself asking questions and being around all the time, but I usually got sympathetic attention. Eventually the chief photographer took pity on me, and gave me an old plate camera which hadn't been used for years and told me to go out and use it.

I went to the local park where the council was dredging and cleaning a lake. I spent half a day taking photographs and the result was a six-picture feature in the group's weekly paper.

That was the beginning, and after that I was given more and more responsible news-photo jobs. I attended night classes intermittently, but believed I could learn more 'on the job' watching, listening to and working alongside the professionals.

After the local paper I moved to work for a local freelance agency, then to a sports agency in London, before going home to freelance for a time. I then moved to my present company as a general photographer. I was allowed to develop the commercial side of the business, changed premises, bought more equipment and so on. Later I became chief photographer and was eventually offered a partnership and became a managing director.

Though I am largely self-taught, I did take every opportunity to widen my experience in the commercial field by studying privately and attending lectures and seminars.

Having spent my entire working life taking mostly press photographs, one of the things that I do dislike about this side of the business is the poor public image that the press seems to have. It is the one thing which has at times made the job uncomfortable. However, the job has offered me variety and challenges. I am very grateful that I have a career which offers me interest every day of my life.

Chapter 3

Institutional and Specialist Photography

Scientific

Generally, a scientific photographer's work is distinct from an industrial photographer's, in that the photographs are used directly to provide information essential to research in a scientific or engineering field. Although the industrial photographer's work is more involved with marketing and publicity there is quite a lot of overlap. Certainly, if you are employed as a scientific photographer, you might also be called upon to do general work, such as taking portraits, shots of premises and social occasions, the production of visual aids, and the illustration of reports, lectures and publications.

There is considerable overlap in terms of training and the type of work done between scientific and medical photography. Very often there may only be two photographers in the department, but in a very big institution there may be as many as 20 staff, some being technicians and assistants. Because much of the work is of a confidential nature in order to main security, it is unlikely that there will be any opportunity for the freelance in this field.

To be a successful scientific photographer calls for patience, accuracy, attention to detail and precision. You may need to work in controlled conditions of a certain temperature or humidity. You may be expected to keep extremely detailed notes on the progress of your photography, and the experimental process and results or conditions at the time. There may be times when you will get very dirty, and you may also be expected to take photographs from uncomfortable and precarious situations at great heights.

Because of the technical nature of much of your work, you will need a good standard of general education. In some fields it may be an advantage to have some training in engineering, applied or pure science. In fact, in some very technical research the scientists themselves have to become conversant with photographic techniques in order to aid their research. Technical and creative flair is a must. You may be expected to adapt techniques and equipment to new situations, and even design photographic equipment specifically for a particular task. Some examples follow of the techniques which a scientific photographer might use.

Holography. A combination of photographic and laser technology which produces a 3-D image in space.

High speed filming. Very short exposures, measured in millionths of a second, are used to analyse processes of very short duration.

Photomicrography. Photography using the microscope.

Macrophotography. Close-up photography witout the use of a compound microscope

Time lapse. Photographs taken at set intervals of time, often over long periods, and used to analyse processes composed of a continuous sequence of events, eg growth, decay etc.

Infra-red and ultra-violet photography. The use of radiation just beyond the limits of the normal visible spectrum to record details which would not be revealed by using visible light.

Aerial photography and stereoscopy. Pairs of photographs taken along parallel axes. When viewed appropriately they reveal 3-D details of ground features, often used in aerial reconnaissance.

There might also be occasions when underwater photography, electron microscopy and many other techniques might be required.

Starting a Career

There are three main employers of scientific photographers: the Civil Service, private industries and universities, although the nationalised industries also rank as employers.

The largest employer of photographers within the Civil Service is the Ministry of Defence. The Civil Service will only accept photographers with BTEC qualifications at HNC or HND level or the SCOTVEC equivalent

For further enquiries you should write to the Civil Service or Ministry of Defence addresses given in Part 2 of this book. Any recruitment to local departments is usually notified to Jobcentres. (For further information see p 35.)

If you are interested in working for private industry, you would be best advised to choose an industry which you think will offer creative and technical scope most suited to your interests and educational background. Unfortunately, at present there is no central organisation which represents photography in private industry. To obtain information on careers it is necessary to write to the individual companies.

In all cases, including university employment, you can obtain up-to-date information by writing to the British Institute of Professional Photographers.

Advertisements for posts most often appear in the *British Journal of Photography*, local press and photographic employment agencies.

Salary

Civil Service

Salary scales (from April 1987)

Basic photographer	£6,388 increasing in 5 yearly increments to £8,370
Senior photographer	£8,097 increasing in 4 yearly increments to £9,523
Principal photographer	£9,949 increasing in 4 yearly increments to £11,465
Chief photographer	£11,637 increasing in 6 yearly increments to £13,962
Superintendent chief photographer	£13,278 increasing in 5 yearly increments to £16,840

University Employment

Photographers are paid according to a technical scale as agreed by the ASTMS.

Trainee salary is age-related, commencing at £3,710 at 16 years and increasing to a maximum of £5,218 at 21 years.

Grade 3	£6,314 - £7,448
Grade 4	£7,140 - £8,266
Grade 5	£7,996 - £9,086
Grade 6	£8,827 - £10,642
Grade 7	£10,276 - £11,643

Medical

Many hospitals now have photographic departments but they vary greatly in the number of personnel employed, depending largely on the size of the institution. There are four main needs for photography. These are to satisfy clinical, research, publication and teaching requirements.

Certainly in this field there is no place for the squeamish. For clinical records you may be required to take photographs of injuries, operations and post mortems. You must be able to deal with people of all ages and temperaments. Remember, too, that many will be very nervous and suffering from serious illness. You must also be familiar with hospital etiquette and prepared to accept its hierarchical structure.

You will be expected to develop and maintain a reasonably up-to-date medical knowledge. You will also be expected to keep abreast of new photographic developments, and to investigate their application to your field. Both of these abilities are essential if you are to be able to discuss and interpret the requirements of doctors, consultants and teaching staff. You may also need to be conversant with video and cine photography and closed-circuit television.

Not only will you have to become expert at techniques such as photomicroscopy, macrophotography, endoscopic photography and the use of infra-red and ultra-violet light sources; on occasions, you may be required to double as a social photographer, recording prize givings and the visits of celebrities. The former may be required as an integral part of research and teaching projects. You will be expected to contribute your own ideas as well.

Sometimes too you may feel that your need for creative fulfilment is constrained by the need for uniformity. For instance, in a long-term project, possibly involving the collation of photographic evidence over a number of years taken by several different photographers, pictures must be taken under controlled conditions, that is, the same scale, lighting, exposure and as near an identical pose as possible. This must be done while ensuring that there is no risk that either you or your equipment transfer infections.

The production of teaching and training aids, such as audio-visual materials will also be one of your responsibilities.

Although medical photographers are not considered to be particularly well paid, their wages compare quite favourably with others in the same sector. Working hours are often organised on a rota basis, and you will be expected to work your share of mornings, evenings and weekends.

Entry requirements are very much the same as for scientific photographers. Sometimes there is a need for technicians, but generally you will begin as a trainee photographer who will be expected to do some darkroom and photofinishing work. When you become a junior photographer, you will be able to do more actual camera work. This will lead through the posts of photographer, where you must be competent in a variety of techniques, eventually to that of chief photographer, where you would be responsible for the department of your institution.

If you begin as a school-leaver, you will be expected to attend college for day release and evening courses. Usually, a high level of general education, especially the sciences, and the successful completion of an appropriate college course will be required.

The majority of school leavers who successfully enter medical photography have five O levels including a science subject and English language. Some entrants also have two A levels. The minimum standard is four O levels.

Organisations

There are a number of representative organisations involved in the maintenance of training and award of qualifications in the scientific and medical fields of photography. These are: the British Institute of Professional Photography (BIPP), the Institute of Medical and Biological Illustration (IMBI), City and Guilds of London Institute, the Business and Technician Education Council (BTEC, and in Scotland, SCOTVEC) and the Council for National Academic Awards (CNAA). There is also a variety of courses for trainees and the opportunity to study for degree and postgraduate qualifications. (Further details are contained in Part 2 of this book.)

If you decide to go to college, first contact the BIPP or the IMBI to make sure that you enrol at a college whose course is approved by these organisations. Vacancies are advertised in the photographic and local press.

Salary

You may be employed as a medical photographer by the National Health Service, by a university or by a joint appointment, that is your salary may be agreed between the NHS and the university.

The latter usually only occurs for fairly senior appointments. University salaries vary widely depending on the particular local authority.

NHS salaries (current for March 1987, pending review)

Basic grade photographer	£5,542–£6,640	Salary increases
Senior medical		in yearly
photographer 1	£6,371–£7,857	increments to
Senior medical		maximum
photographer 2	£7,156–£9,044	shown for
Chief photographer	£9,221–£10,394	grade.

There are two grades of trainee photographer and the salary increases with the age of the entrant. The minimum salary is for entry at 16.

Grade A	Grade B
£3,293–£4,649	£3,494–£4,834

Educational and Other Institutions

There are many institutions which are involved directly or indirectly with education. These include: museums, trade associations, national parks departments, charities, advisory councils, education authorities, libraries and many more. Photographers are employed to teach photography in colleges and in schools run by manufacturers and major retailers. There are also opportunities to teach part-time photographic courses in many schools and some colleges. Certainly, when it comes to teaching photography, it is best if you can draw on knowledge gained while working in the field.

The number of photographers employed depends very much on the size and activity of the institution in question. It may employ just one all-rounder or a staff of a dozen or more. Museums often use a vast amount of photographic material, with even more resource material stored in their picture library. In a small museum, you might be expected to be able to photograph a small exhibit, maintain the picture library and take snaps at the Christmas party!

There are also many other government and independent organisations which exist to document, research and promote certain subjects. One of the advantages of working for an institution is that it is not difficult to find one which specialises in a subject which is of particular interest to you.

Once again, in this field of photography there may be considerable overlap between it and, say, the scientific field. If you work in a university or in a museum, you may be required to use specialist and sophisticated photographic equipment. Your work may involve macrophotography and photomicrography, for instance. You will, therefore, be expected to have a good general level of education. In fact, this field has similar entry requirements to those for scientific photography.

Starting a Career

Some institutions may offer trainee posts to school-leavers, but preference may be given to those who have completed a course of full-time study at a college. School-leavers, if accepted, will be expected to attend day release or evening classes at college. If you wish to reach a senior position, experience in the industrial and commercial sectors may be necessary. Depending on the institution, this bias may be more towards the scientific side of photography. Recognised qualifications, such as City and Guilds or a certificate of the British Institute of Professional Photography, may also be required.

Some vacancies are advertised in the trade press and by photographic employment agencies.

Certainly, if you are interested in working for a particular organisation, you should write to it at an early stage to find out exactly what requirements are expected for its photography department. (See pp 35 and 25 for Civil Service and scientific opportunities.)

Salary

Salaries vary enormously depending on the employer. The only salaries which are consistent nationwide are those of the Civil Service. Local government salaries vary from one authority to another, as do those for private organisations. To obtain specific information on this matter, you should write directly to the organisation or authority concerned.

Case Study

David has followed a circuitous route to his current position of *graphics officer* for a county council. However, it shows that a wide experience can be an advantage in terms of career flexibility.

I attended a Manchester school for boys which tended to produce engineers and scrap metal spivs, rather than academic students destined for higher education. I was further frustrated because I was artistic, something which was rather frowned upon.

Despite a variety of problems I managed to go to art school. I chose graphic design as my major subject and photography as my minor subject. I thought that each would serve the other, and, as it turned out, it was a wise choice.

Maybe it is important to point out at this juncture that I had no qualifications whatsoever. I ducked out at O levels, A levels and even the final diploma year at art school – although I would not necessarily condone the fact.

Before the end of my course, I received an offer of employment with one of Manchester's top advertising agencies which I accepted. They were a great bunch of people to work for and I learned an awful lot. In fact, I had to relearn most of what I had been taught at art school.

My post with the agency was trainee graphic designer. However, because of my interest in photography I began to spend more and more time in the darkroom and studio. At the time I was 18 years old. At first I did reducing and enlarging of headlines and copy, as well as helping in studio and location photography.

I still wanted to be a photographere in my own right, so when I saw an advertisement for a police photographer with the local constabulary I jumped at the opportunity. At the interview the chief photographer chatted to me for some time about the emotional and mental strain of the job. I was also asked to produce a number of prints in a set time in the darkroom. When I emerged 20 minutes later, he seemed to be pleased with my speed and ability. I had my new job and a salary of £13 per week!

Initially the job consisted of printing negatives taken by the two principal photographers. A typical selection included portraits of villains from the morning court, the previous night's fingerprint haul and multiple sets of photographic evidence for juries. On the Friday of my first week with the Police, my boss decided to 'throw me in at the deep end' and took me down to the city mortuary to photograph a post mortem on an 18-month-old baby.

This experience heralded the beginning of two-and-a-half years of similar experiences varying in degrees of grisliness! I went into that job as a 22-year-old boy and came out a 24-year-old man!

The most challenging aspect of the job was the fact that at a scene of a crime you only had one shot at it. It was essential to know exactly what you were doing.

Ironically, my first assignment was concerning the death of a child and so too was my last. This particular murder of two children finished me off, and I had to put an end to my 'hardening life'.

During the next six months I worked for a commercial

photographic studio, and then helped with the design and production of four industrial magazines. Eventually I became a managing director of two of these publications. Photography played very little part in my existence there and although the position I held was 'heady', I felt that my talents were stagnating because I was becoming a 'delegator' rather than a 'doer'.

I became increasingly unhappy and began to look around. I obtained a job with the local county council as an assistant public relations officer. It involved writing press releases, talking to the press and media, writing and taking pictures for the local airport's newsletter and a little bit of graphics.

After a while I began to do less writing, and the demand for my graphics soared to 100 per cent of my time as it is today. Shortly afterwards I was promoted to the newly created post of graphics officer.

I am a 'one man band' serving 13 of the 17 departments. I produce not only designs for posters, books, brochures, advertising campaigns and exhibitions, but also photography for the above tasks. I also photograph chairmen's visits and official functions, make audiovisual presentations and do various other duties which arise from time to time.

Recently we have jumped into the video business and I am now in charge of this aspect of the job.

I find my present position offers plenty of excitement and challenge. I also love the interest and accolades it generates. My convoluted career history also shows that strings of qualifications are not necessarily required to open doors to well-paid jobs. I would advocate hard work, sincerity, integrity and a very good sense of humour as the essential ingredients for a successful career.

Photographic Education

Most teachers of photography are employed by institutions of higher and further education. Their job is to train the technicians and photographers of the future. To be able to do this competently, they must have a good knowledge of photography past and present. The best teachers have lived and worked as professionals and can tell the students what life as a photographer or technician is really like. At present, a great many students are leaving college without a real appreciation of what it is like to make a living from photography.

Staff are employed as lecturers, instructors, technicians and heads of departments, and may be full-time or part-time. A good introduction to the teaching side of photography can be gained by taking occasional night classes. One can also learn a lot by watching others teach. This type of experience can often be gained by being actively involved in a professional photographic association.

As a teacher, you will be expected to have and maintain close connections with professional photographers and associations. Above all, you should have a genuine interest in teaching and developing other people's careers and talents. You will also have to cope with a large amount of paperwork, marking and setting of examinations, and will have to be able to plan relevant courses within a set budget.

Technicians will be expected to have City and Guilds qualifications or their equivalent. You will need to have had studio or laboratory experience.

Starting a Career

For work as a technician you will need a secondary standard of education with at least one science. However, many colleges have their own particular requirements. Some specify an A level. City and Guilds courses are currently under review, with the assistance of many of the professional associations, and new syllabuses may commence around September 1988.

You can approach getting a job in one of two ways. Either you could find a college which would take you on as a school-leaver, or you could attend college and do a City and Guilds course. For details see Chapter 9. In either case jobs are most often advertised in the photographic or local press. It is interesting to note that at present 80 per cent of jobs advertised in photography are for technicians.

Obviously if you are interested in teaching photography, you would first need to have a good general knowledge and experience of working in commercial photography. However, to gain teaching experience one could begin by taking night classes, say at a local secondary school. There is no possibility of simply going straight into college lecturing. This should only be done by those who have a strong desire to teach, and really have knowledge and experience to impart which they have gained through working in the field.

Salary

Salary depends on the pay scale relevant to the grade of work.

Civil Service

In the government sector, a major employer of photographers is the Civil Service. Recruitment for photographic posts is undertaken locally by departments that have vacancies to offer. Jobcentres are normally notified of these vacancies.

Within the Civil Service, the Ministry of Defence is the largest employer of photographic staff. All grades of employment are now classed simply as 'photographer'. There is no age limit on entry but candidates must have BTEC HNC/HND or SCOTVEC equivalent qualifications. All promotions to higher grades are on a competitive basis after one year's service in the lower grade. On rare occasions, when suitable candidates cannot be found within the existing Civil Service, there may be open competition for direct entry to higher grades.

The photographers working for the Ministry of Defence embrace almost all available photographic techniques in the fields of still, cine, television and graphic artwork in support of printing units. Their work ranges from straightforward public relations jobs to the more obscure scientific applications. However, most of the work is carried out in support of other functions and services, and very little pure photographic research is undertaken.

In the Civil Service your work may sometimes concern matters relating to national security. For this reason, you can expect that your background may be investigated and there are strict entry conditions related to nationality. For more information related to employment in the Ministry of Defence and the Civil Service Commission, please write to the address given in Part 2 of this book. (See also p 27.)

Armed Forces

Photographers are used in all three branches of the armed forces. However, no one can enter either the Army or Navy solely to be a photographer. You must have a genuine interest in service life and be prepared to enter on a completely different grade. You may have the opportunity, once within the service, to apply for selection for photographic duties. Selection is fierce and competition is very tough. If you fail to be selected, you will have to be prepared to continue your service career in another field.

Army

Once qualified in another field, Army photographers take an initial ten-week course at RAOC Blackdown, with a further opportunity to attend a seven-month course at Cosford. Most of their work is of the public relations variety, with some specialised duties such as technical and aerial photography.

Girls in the WRAC are not trained as photographers. At present the only opportunity is a casual use of photographs by your unit, that is, any photography you did would most likely be on an amateur basis.

Navy

Photographers in the Navy are part of the Fleet Air Arm. After a minimum two years' service, you could apply for training as a photographer. After training, you would be expected to undertake work both above and below the surface of the sea. There may be aerial work and you would be expected to handle still, cine and video cameras. About half of your work would concern weaponry and the rest would come under the general heading of public relations.

Women in the WRENS have very similar duties but they do not go to sea for long periods. However, they can enter the service directly at the photographer grade. Photographers in the Navy can theoretically proceed to the rank of lieutenant commander; although there is no WREN photographic officer rank at present this could change.

RAF

The primary purpose of photography in the RAF is to aid aerial reconnaissance. However, although you might be involved in the fitting, servicing and testing of the cameras, they would be operated by the aircraft's pilot.

Air photographic processors are involved in the high speed processing, sometimes in less than 30 minutes, of miles of black and white film. Very little colour film is used for this work.

In 1977 the RAF began to recruit both men and women directly into ground photography. This more closely resembles the work a civilian photographer would do, as much of the work concerns public relations; a significant amount of the film produced is in colour.

It should be stated that recruitment to the armed forces varies considerably from year to year. For up-to-date information on the situation you should consult the appropriate local services careers office.

It is also possible to gain direct entry to the photographic interpretation branch. Officers and NCOs are employed as photographic interpreters, and use their skill, knowledge and experience to interpret aerial photographs. The accumulation of intelligence data requires a methodical, analytical approach and painstaking care. Such positions are also offered by the Civil Service Commission.

Photographers within the armed forces whose work is very limited or specialised may, on leaving the services, find it difficult to obtain comparable jobs within the commercial and industrial sector.

Starting a Career

Army

Most major towns and cities have recruiting centres which can give up-to-date information. You need to have at least three passes at GCE O level (CSE grade 1) or GCSE equivalent, one of which must be maths or chemistry. Before you are accepted you must also pass the entrance examination. Before going on to training at Cosford, you must first qualify as a supply controller or staff clerk with the RAOC.

To work as a photographic processor, you should first be accepted into the Royal Engineers. To qualify as a survey print technician or a survey photographic technician, you will have to pass an aptitude test before going on to train at the School of Military Survey, Hermitage, Newbury. Your future promotions and salary would depend on the successful completion of training, and gaining the necessary qualifications.

Navy

To join the Navy, boys need to be at least 16 years of age and girls 17 years of age, and to have left school. You would be expected to have a minimum of CSE grade 2 or equivalent in maths and English. In the beginning, you would be a naval airman in the Fleet Air Arm. Once you had become a leading airman you could apply to do photography. Evidence of previous interest and knowledge of photography would be useful, plus a good general level of education. There is no opportunity to do photography if you join as a trainee officer.

Wrens

You can enter at a minimum age of 17½ years. You would be expected to have a knowledge of physics and chemistry and to have at least an O level or CSE grade 1 in mathematics. A previous knowledge or interest in photography would be an advantage.

RAF

The minimum age of entry is 16 years for boys and 17 years for girls but there is no minimum educational standard. Instead, it is necessary to sit and pass an IQ test.

There are four fields in which photography is used: ground photography (mostly public relations and similar work), air photographic processing, air cartography and plotting/aerial photography. The former two require a knowledge of mechanics and electronics, while the latter need an educational background biased to the arts and crafts. To become a photographic interpreter's assistant you would have to pass specialist aptitude tests and demonstrate an adequate level of neatness and drawing skills.

Salary

Army

Salary would be as for a normal soldier. You would begin at £103.32 gross per week. This assumes that you are 17½ years old and have signed on for three years. If you were accepted into the Royal Engineers, you would receive trade pay (starting at £113.47 a week after basic training) which would increase depending on training, qualifications and rank.

Navy

Wages vary depending on the length of engagement with the Navy. The minimum salary for a leading airman is £186.20 a week for a three-year engagement. The minimum salary for a nine-year engagement is £188.30. Wage increases depend on qualifications and rank attained, for example a warrant officer earns £286.51 a week.

WRENS

Salary on entry is £76.37 per week if younger than 17½ years, and £100.94 if older, rising to a maximum of £297.15 per week as a fleet chief.

RAF
Salaries depend on age and period of engagement. For example, on entry at 16½ for a six-year engagement, the minimum salary is £64.33 gross per week. This rises after six months and the passing of exams to £78.12. The maximum salary at 18 years, but for a nine-year engagement, is £108.57.

Police and Forensic Science

This is another job which is definitely not for the squeamish. Having said this, you must also be prepared for some of your work to be fairly mundane. Some of the time you will be expected to make prints and slides of specimens and artwork. You will also be required to help in the production of audio-visual displays, and material which is to be used as part of training programmes.

The City of London Force uses serving police officers, but many photographers are civilian employees. You would have to check with your regional police headquarters to find out what happens in your area.

Photographic work in the Police Force comes broadly under three headings: studio, outdoor and darkroom.

In the studio, the photographer may have to copy fingerprints which have been 'lifted' and labelled by an officer investigating a crime. You may also have to photograph small objects such as stolen items, weapons and guns. These photographs may be later produced in court and used as part of the evidence. At other times, you may be expected to record the injuries of people who have been the victims of assault.

Very often, you will be one of the first called upon to take photographs at the scene of a crime. You may also have to visit the mortuary, take photographs of the scene of an accident or photograph admissions to prison. You may be called in as part of a surveillance team to record the movements of a suspect. In many of these situations you must be able to work rapidly and without being noticed. Most of your work will be in black and white, with some colour and possibly a requirement to use a cine or video camera.

In a large photographic unit a junior will often be responsible for the darkroom work, but a more experienced photographer will be expected to supervise. Photographs which are to be used as evidence cannot be retouched. You will also be expected to complete all the paperwork and keep notes concerning any photographs which may be used in court. On occasions, you will be expected to appear in court in connection with such photographs.

Specialist photographic techniques, such as macrophotography and photomicrography, are required to record and compare textile fibres, hairs, dust, rifle marks on a bullet, handwriting and typescript. Infra-red techniques may be used to examine bloodstains, powder burns resulting from the use of firearms and to detect fake paintings. Fluorescence methods are used to detect erasures and forgeries. It should be emphasised that much of your work will not be artistic; a faithful record of evidence or events is all that is required.

In return for having to be on call, and occasionally working unsocial hours including shifts, you will have secure employment, with good pay and conditions, a high salary compared to similarly qualified photographers in other sectors, and job opportunities available all over the country.

Starting a Career

Entry requirements and training vary from one force to another. Some, including the Metropolitan Police Force, take school-leavers as trainee assistant photographers. The minimum requirement is three O levels or equivalent, including English, mathematics and a science. Some forces prefer the City and Guilds 744 and 745, or an appropriate qualification endorsed by the British Institute of Professional Photography.

Salary

Most police photographers are employed by local government for which there is no national pay scale. For specific information, you should contact the police in the area in which you wish to work. However, photographers working for Scotland Yard are employed by the Civil Service, and their salaries can be expected to have a London weighting. In general, salary depends on experience, qualifications and age.

Case Study

Philip has been a *police photographer* since leaving school at 18 years of age. Now, almost 20 years later, he is chief photographer with one of the provincial forces. Although still a 'civilian' employee, officially termed non-police personnel, he heads a photographic department and is experienced in forensic science, fingerprints and, of course, photography.

Had I not been able to become a photographer, I would have joined the Police Force anyway. I was always interested in police work but was also a keen photographer. I have been lucky to be able to combine both interests in one career.

I began as a darkroom technician and assistant photographer with a small provincial force. Besides receiving specialist in-house training, I attended day release courses for City and Guilds and Institute of Incorporated Photographers qualifications. I also learnt a tremendous amount from the other photographic officers to whom I was attached. I was promoted to photographer when I was 21 years of age. One's progress is continually monitored by the department, you must come up to scratch in both your external and internal assessments.

A short while later I transferred to Scotland Yard, still as a photographer. During my service there I was promoted to senior photographer and also received training in fingerprinting and forensic science.

When some of the forces underwent reorganisation in 1972, brand new departments known as 'scenes of crime' departments were instigated. By this time, the experience and qualifications I had gained were very appropriate to this type of work, and I moved to one of these departments as a scenes of crime officer. Two years later, I became a senior scenes of crime officer and after another four years I became the chief photographer.

I enjoy the variety of work this job offers, it certainly isn't nine to five, and I feel it gives a lot of job satisfaction. We handle all sorts of equipment from 35mm to technical 5 x 4 inches, video, heat detection, image intensification, and are becoming increasingly involved in fibre optics and the latest image recording and transmission technologies. We have our own television studio and do a huge variety of still photography. Other assignments include aerial studies, still-life shots of stolen property, portraiture, surveillance work and 'creative' advertising type shots for police road safety campaigns.

We also enjoy a job security which is hard to find these days. There are excellent sporting and social facilities, and help may be given in meeting removal and legal expenses incurred in job transferral. Trainees receive expert tuition and we use all the best equipment.

However, opposed to this I have to be available always 'on call', 24 hours a day, 365 days a year. I work in a very disciplined structure and have to accept a fair amount of routine. There is no such thing as a 'typical' day, but to give you some idea my day begins at eight in the morning when I check the night logs and do any appropriate follow up. I check the department's work flow and discuss any problems with my assistants. I also usually have a fair amount of internal and external correspondence to cope with.

Much of my day is spent on administrative duties, planning, paperwork, ensuring that this complex department runs smoothly.

There are also important duties such as interviewing trade representatives. This is necessary because I must be aware of new developments in both equipment and materials.

Despite some of the drawbacks of this job, there are far more people who want to work in the photographic department than there are vacancies. Recently we advertised one trainee job and received hundreds of applications.

The most important thing that we look for in a potential trainee is a photographic aptitude. I feel that aptitude is as important as qualifications. If someone has an aptitude for the job he can be moulded and trained. One of the problems we find with people who come to us with college diplomas is that they expect too much. They expect to be given the best jobs and don't want to do the more menial tasks. Even if a person is experienced, we consider that it takes about two to four years to make him a useful photographer. People tend to forget just what a specialised job this is. Very often, in the case of a murder or serious road accident, your photography has to be absolutely right, and unbiased, first time. You don't have a second chance; if you suddenly realised that you had made a mistake, by the time you had returned to the scene the road would have been cleared and the victims removed.

There is scope for women in the job, especially when dealing with female injury cases and children. The job is physically hard, though, and so there tends to be more men than women.

If I were to sum up the qualities required to be a good police photographer, I would list as most important: photographic aptitude, a sense of humour, confidence (this often comes with experience) discipline and dedication, a methodical approach to problems, physical fitness and a willingness to learn.

Chapter 4

Photojournalism and Press Photography

Press

The good press photographer must have an 'eye' for news, in much the same way as a journalist must have a 'nose' for a good story. He must be able to interpret a story, and decide rapidly how he can take advantage of the best opportunities to take pictures. The most difficult aspect of the press photographer's job is that he has to be able to sum up a complicated situation with just one monochrome photograph. He rarely has second chances and must be able to take the required shot very quickly. Indeed, speed is of the essence. If your photographs are not ready for the printing deadline, they are very unlikely to be of any use.

Most press photographers commence work with a provincial newspaper. Here the requirement is mostly for material of regional interest, for example topical stories and human interest features. The photographer must be versatile, and he may be expected to photograph a lot of very mundane events and retain the enthusiasm to inject 'something special' into every shot.

There is intense competition for jobs in the transition from a provincial to a national newspaper. Here the work is much more news oriented. The photographer must work under greater pressure and carry more responsibility, because the prestige of the paper's name is at stake.

Only highly reliable, talented and resourceful photographers make this difficult transition. The work is tough and can be dangerous. On an overseas assignment, you may have to cope with poor food and accommodation, physical and mental stress, and extreme difficulty in transporting your pictures from an isolated area to the newspaper to meet the deadlines. At the same time, you have to out-think and outmanoeuvre both the subject of your photography and the competition from other publications.

Press photography involves working unsocial hours but is fairly well paid, particularly if you are employed by a national paper.

Starting a Career

None of the national newspapers take on school-leavers or college graduates as trainee photographers. Training is only undertaken by the provincial papers.

If you wish to apply for press photography training, you should write direct to the editor of a regional or local newspaper for employment as an indentured trainee. The names and addresses of regional and local newspapers can be obtained from *Benn's Media Directory* or *Willing's Press Guide*, copies of which should be available in local reference libraries.

For direct entry the minimum educational standards are:

1. Five O level passes at A, B, or C, or
2. One A level and four O level passes, or
3. Two A levels and two O levels.

All passes should be in different subjects. GCSE equivalents will apply from summer 1988. Alternatively the NCTJ may adjudicate to decide if previous work experience is acceptable.

There is a full-time course for potential press photographers at Richmond College of Further Education, Sheffield which has been arranged by the newspaper industry. The course is run in conjunction with the National Council for the Training of Journalists, the industry's official training organisation. The council also organises the selection of students.

This full-time course is an alternative method of entry into press photography training. Most trainee photographers join provincial newspapers direct without going through the course and, during three-year indenture, attend block release courses at the Sheffield college. A limited number, however, are selected for the full-time course which is normally followed by 2¼ years' indenture on a provincial newspaper. Vocational experience during indenture, including taking the NCTJ press photography proficiency test, completes the training after the course.

To be considered for the course, you need at least one A level and four O level certificates (including English language) in different subjects, and to be under 20 years of age on 1 September of the year the course starts. Students sitting GCE/

GCSE examinations early in the year are eligible, although final acceptance depends on gaining the required number of passes. The O levels must be either grade A, B or C. Grade 1 CSE equates with an O level.

Students who pass the course examinations are assisted by the NCTJ and the college in obtaining employment as trainee press photographers on provincial newspapers. Further details on the course and the selection of entrants are included in Part 2 of this book. Further information can be obtained by writing to the NCTJ and the Newspaper Society Training Department (see p 91).

Salary

Entrants under 24 years of age on regional and local newspapers have to undergo indentured training. Starting wages at 19 years of age and under, depending on newspaper pay group, range from £74.70 to £105.83 per week, at 20–23 years of age from £80.93 to £112.05, graduates under 24 years of age receive from £93.38 to £112.05 per week.

In the case of direct entrants, after satisfactory completion of six months' probation, all these rates rise by an average of about £6 per week.

Trainees from pre-entry and postgraduate courses start at rates of pay approximately £10 per week higher than the figures shown above. After satisfactory completion of three months' probation, rates rise by a further £6 per week on average.

Starting salaries for qualified staff range from £124.50 to £146 per week, depending on the pay group of the weekly or daily newspaper concerned.

After two years' qualified service this increases from £135.25 to £159.75 per week, and after five years' service from £140 to £171.50. Local agreements and merit money often supplement qualified rates.

Agencies

News and press agencies do employ their own photographers, although a lot of their material is also supplied by freelance photographers. Much of the advice and job description applied to press photography is relevant here. The same aptitudes are required, and with the job comes the same pressure, competition and working conditions. Press agencies will only consider recommended photographers who have appropriate experience.

Editorial

Editorial photography is used to illustrate and accompany information in magazines, periodicals and technical journals. Generally one's work is concentrated on a particular subject, for example, motor bikes, cars, hi-fi and so on. Of course, a photographer has to look at different aspects of a subject. Sometimes the photography will be done by a member of the staff, but more often a freelance is assigned for particular jobs or is kept on a retainer. The photographer may need to work to a brief, although this is generally not as tight as in advertising. Obviously if you are a staff photographer, you will enjoy more security and less pressure than a freelance. A freelance who can both write and generate his own editorial ideas may find that he is able to enjoy a steadier income than someone who is solely a photographer.

Photojournalism

A photojournalist is not a photographer who can write as well as take pictures. He is a photographer who is able to tell a story *with* pictures. In the present economic climate, magazines are very limited for space and the opportunities for this sort of photography are limited. Even the Sunday supplement magazines, once a big purchaser of this type of material, tend to use features which require a minimum of illustration. Of course, a very exclusive set of pictures which are especially topical or newsworthy will sell. However, such material is often only obtainable by an established photographer who has the necessary reputation or contacts.

This is a field which can be entered by the novice with a good eye for a picture. However, it is very much the province of the freelance. There are virtually no opportunities for 'true' staff photojournalists. There are more opportunities for this type of work in America and on the Continent but competition is extreme. To have any chance of success, you need a remarkable portfolio and proven experience with major publishers throughout the world.

Obviously it is an advantage in this field if you can write well. Also, you must be able to generate and sell ideas before you actually commence work. Then you must be able both to organise and carry out your project to a successful conclusion.

Freelance Photography

A freelance photographer is one who offers his services for hire. Many of the careers already discussed are largely the province of the freelance. Very often he is a specialist known for working in a particular field with a distinctive style. There are also many general practice freelance photographers who may work in the press, commercial and industrial sectors, as well as doing weddings, portraits and so on.

Many magazines and periodicals find that financial constraints make it economical to hire only freelance photographers. For instance, the colour supplements use no staff photographers, all photographic material is generated by freelancers.

The difficulties involved in establishing oneself as a freelance photographer should not be underestimated. It may take ten years for you to establish a 'name'. From the outset you may need facilities and equipment which you cannot possibly afford. At the same time, you are trying to compete with established photographers who have all the facilities which you lack.

This is a hard training ground which has produced some superb British photographers. In the early days of your business you will need to be a 'jack-of-all-trades'. You will be secretary, telephonist, marketing manager, accountant and darkroom assistant as well as photographer. You must have the confidence to sell yourself to art buyers and picture editors. You will need to spend months showing people your portfolio and tramping the streets.

You will have to decide whether you want to train at a college or learn through experience. One thing that you should bear in mind when choosing a course of training is that very few truly prepare novices for the hardships of life as a freelance. If the artist does not have a flair for business, he will not survive for long.

Starting a Career

In the field of photojournalism and press photography, most openings are advertised in the trade press, newspapers, and photographic employment agencies. It is not a particularly secure area of employment as the recession has brought hard times for most of the publishing world.

Salary

If you are employed full-time, this has to be negotiated between you and the publisher. Most often you will be paid on publication. The payment will either be according to a day rate, or space used in the publication. Once again, those rates are normally negotiated.

Case Study

Peter, a *freelance photographer*, began his business two years ago having left a fairly secure but predictable job as a teacher.

> I felt for a long time that I had something to offer photographically. I have had absolutely no training, but when I was young belonged to a school photography club which taught me most of the elementary things about developing and processing. Since then I have just learnt from my mistakes and by doing a lot of reading about the subject. Frankly, I don't see any reason why you need to go to college to learn a mastery of the technical side of photography.
>
> Most of my earnings at present come from the selling of photojournalistic-type features. I have also done some advertising work and supplied illustrations for books. I am a bit limited in finding more advertising assignments, in that I don't have access to a studio, and in fact could probably not afford one at the moment.
>
> I am pretty lucky in that I am able to write reasonably well. From the point of view of selling features to various magazines, it gives me an advantage and also means I can earn more cash from a job.
>
> Some people would probably regard me as having been very successful so far, considering I have only been going for such a short time. I have had major features published in all the British colour supplements, Time-Life publications and in Europe. I now realise that I've only just begun to scratch the surface of success.
>
> When I first started I thought that once I had been published in a few major publications I would have 'made it'. For instance, I thought that if I had a feature in a Time-Life publication I would have 'arrived'. I've learnt that this idea of 'making it' is really a myth. For a long time, a photographer is considered to be only as good as the last job. It actually takes time and consistent effort to gain recognition.
>
> Working and existing as a freelance photographer is a little like being a professional tightrope walker. You're constantly having to re-assess what you're doing. You have to make quick decisions based on intuition, but stay steady at other times despite the ups and downs of life. You need to be balanced artistically, temperamentally and from the business point of view. Survival is the name of the game!

One of the exciting things about this business is that it requires such a unique blend of talents. Obviously you have to be a very good photographer. At the same time you have to be good at selling yourself. It's vital to have the right manner whether talking on the telephone, seeing someone or writing a letter. You need to be open and to be able to absorb ideas from all different sorts of quarters. You must be able to organise and coordinate many different factors to bring a job to a successful conclusion. Above all, you should try to be professional in everything that you do.

What you never get used to is the nagging sense of insecurity. It takes a long time before you can feel 'safe', and until then you keep looking over your shoulder. In fact, I suspect that if you lost that sense of insecurity it might also remove the spur which keeps you creative. All of us are inclined to be lazy. That sense of impending starvation is probably necessary to keep you really sharp.

Picture Libraries, Editors and Researchers

Picture libraries and agencies keep large stocks of colour and black and white photographs and sell them on behalf of the photographer. For the service, they charge a commission which is usually about 50 per cent of sales. Picture libraries employ secretaries, telephonists and specialist staff like dupers, printers and others. This is quite a specialist field, and experience is more important than training. Generally, you would begin as an office junior. You need a great interest in photographs, photographers and photography if you wish to progress.

Photographic editors usually work for a publisher. Their job is to choose the best photographs for publication from a bewildering selection. You will have to work to deadlines; there is considerable pressure for those employed by the press and periodicals. In some cases, you may have to commission a photographer to provide particular illustrations for a feature. You will need to know who is the best available specialist, and be able to contact him or her quickly. You may also have to contact picture libraries or specialist researchers to find photographs for you.

A picture researcher is employed to find photographs, often of a very specialist nature, for publication. You need good contacts in the trade, and should build up your own directory of photographers and libraries.

To be a successful picture researcher or editor, you must have a very good memory for a picture. You need to know exactly where you saw that 'ideal' shot while browsing through a magazine a year ago. You need to keep up to date with all forms of photography and a wide range of publications. It would be very embarrassing if you republished pictures in your magazine which had been used even as much as two years ago, even if at that time you were not working for the publication.

For further information contact: Arona Shene, Chairwoman of the Society of Picture Researchers and Editors (SPREd), BM259, London WC1N 3XX.

Chapter 5

Photofinishing

Introduction

The photofinishing trade caters for the hundreds of thousands of films which are sent by amateurs to processing laboratories all over the country. However, there is a distinction to be drawn between these laboratories and the specialist laboratories which cater for the needs of the professional. You will see the distinction more clearly after reading the next chapter on professional photographic laboratories.

Competition for trade between photofinishing laboratories has become increasingly cut-throat. This has meant that pressure on the industry, manufacturers and suppliers has led to increased automation of all processes. Nowadays in a modern, fully equipped laboratory machines are almost completely automatic. Microprocessors control virtually all the operations involved in processing film and printing from negatives.

This change in the nature of the industry has resulted in a major change in the employment situation and its associated career structure. There is now far less need for photographic technicians, and an increased requirement for people with computer and programming skills and experience. This represents the major difference which has developed between photofinishers and specialist photographic laboratories.

At present, there is no really appropriate training course offered by a photographic college which would fit a trainee specifically to operate the new 'chip' technology processing machinery. Nevertheless, a college training course would furnish you with an appreciation of photographic materials and their characteristics, which would be beyond the scope of a computer programmer. If you are really interested in the technical or specialist side of photofinishing, you might be better advised to seek a career with one of the manufacturers of photographic materials and processors, or one of the professional photographic laboratories.

It should also be added that this is one employment area which often seems to have a predominance of women. There are often opportunities for employment on a temporary basis which is often of more interest to women. The demand for photofinishing varies seasonally, with a high peak in the summer when a laboratory may process up to three times the average throughput of material which occurs during the post-Christmas period. It is during this summer peak that there is often a need for temporary staff.

Within the photofinishing trade, there are two main areas of skill and experience. These are the technical and man-management fields. However, separate from this is the need for ancillary employees, who can move into the technical area, and this will be dealt with first.

Ancillary Staff

Unlike a photographic studio, where a young assistant may also find himself to be the sweep and tea-boy, staff are specifically employed to do these jobs. Obviously, you do not need high educational qualifications and there is also room here for temporary employment. Sometimes these jobs are available during school holidays, when the laboratory usually finds itself under the greatest workload. This might allow a school pupil, considering employment in such a job, to gain some insight into the profession. However, it should be stressed that it is highly unlikely that he would be entrusted with any photographic work. It might be possible, at a later stage, to become a production worker, which will involve the handling of photographic materials after a suitable amount of training and experience has been gained.

Production Workers

Production workers include the photographic machine operators. There is scope here for the employment of school-leavers with a good general and scientific education. Initially, most of your work would involve fairly mundane tasks such as preparing and identifying work for the different processes. In fact, on average about two-thirds of the people employed by a photofinishing laboratory do just this type of work. You must be able to differentiate between the different types and sizes of film, they may need to be processed in different ways in different machines. At the other end of the production line are those who pack the film and prints into wallets, and whose responsibility it is that the customers' 'snaps' return to them safely.

Once you have shown your ability to do this type of work, you may become a machine operator. About one-third of production workers do this work. Even though most of the machines are very nearly fully automatic and controlled by 'chips', this is a very responsible job. You are there to make sure that nothing goes wrong. You must be able to anticipate problems and ensure that you know what to do in any eventuality.

The training for this type of work is all in-service. Some of the machines used for processing cost up to £250,000. There is, therefore, close cooperation between the manufacturers of the machinery and the laboratory, and between them they ensure that the operator is correctly trained.

You will be responsible to either a senior operator or a supervisor who has considerable experience in your area. It is possible, if you can prove your reliability, that you too may one day be promoted to such a position.

Many photofinishing laboratories specialise in either black and white or colour processing. However, if you work in a laboratory which is involved in both types of work, it is most likely that you would still specialise in just one machine operation.

Technicians

There are two main categories of technician; engineers who are involved in the maintenance of the machines, and quality controllers who monitor the machines and processes to ensure that they are operating to the correct standards and peak efficiency.

Because of the increasingly sophisticated and technical nature of the machinery, one needs less and less real photographic expertise, and much more appreciation of computers, figures and a readiness to accept the new technology. Soon, all processing machines will be entirely automatic, controlled and monitored by computers. The machine will be able to diagnose its own faults and apply the appropriate remedy.

However, even in a very large laboratory there may be a

requirement for a conventional enlarger and operator. If so, an experienced and trained technician will be needed.

Engineers are usually accepted who have minimum basic training. They will then be trained further by the machine manufacturers on behalf of the laboratory. This is partly because there is such a large variety of processing machines available, and because no college at the moment offers a suitable training course.

Experienced engineers may become quality controllers. They have to liaise very closely with the manufacturers of the machine and the photographic material. Test films and prints have to be processed and analysed to check that everything is working correctly. They must also make sure that the prints and films which are going to be returned to people are of the necessary high standard. This work involves considerable experience, and the ability to make quite difficult decisions based on scientific and subjective criteria.

Supervisors and Senior Operators

Both these jobs have already been mentioned briefly. Supervisors and senior operators are responsible for seeing that machine operators do their jobs correctly. At the same time, they must be able to give advice and help their staff to gain experience. As a supervisor, you will also have to liaise with the engineers and quality controllers to ensure that your machines can be working at their best during peak times.

In a large laboratory there may be a shift system in operation. During the peak periods there will be more shifts than at the slack time. The supervisors and senior operators will occasionally have to work shifts too. They must also be responsible for the smooth running of their section or department even during those times when they are not on shift.

These days a supervisor is more and more someone who has proven man-management skills and experience, although it is also important that he has a wide appreciation of photographic principles.

It is possible for a production worker to eventually be promoted to supervisor or senior operator. However, because so many of the production jobs are highly specialised, they may not necessarily give you the right experience to rise to higher positions. It is important to be aware of this if you are thinking of making photofinishing a career. In particular, you may not gain the man-management skills necessary for management.

Management

Increasingly, promotion to these posts is governed by your ability to manage a resource. It has been said that it does not really matter whether that resource is photographs or cakes. The management skills are still the same. What you must be able to do is to manage the business so efficiently that you receive value for money from the millions of pounds worth of machinery. A manager has to be able to analyse how the business can be made more streamlined and the machinery used more effectively. You and your supervisory team may have to work long hours, sometimes as many as 50–60 hours per week, to achieve this.

It is important to emphasise that this industry is very different from what it was even ten years ago. One machine without an operator may now produce more than 20,000 prints per hour! This degree of automation allows a minimum work force to be highly cost effective in terms of its output.

This change in the nature of the industry has radically affected its career structure. Once again, even ten years ago, a school-leaver working as a general assistant could have expected that one day he might rise through the ranks to be a laboratory manager. This type of career structure is rapidly disappearing within the industry, unless you are lucky enough to have a manager who is unusually sympathetic. You are unlikely to receive the sort of training and experience working as a machine operator or production worker to fit you for a managerial position. Considerable dichotomy is developing between the technical and man-management sides of the business.

Starting a Career

Openings in photofinishing are usually advertised in the trade press, newspapers and less often by photographic employment agencies. Advertisements may also appear in the local Jobcentres, especially for temporary employment.

Although this is a growing industry it is still fairly small. Many managers looking for supervisors, senior operators and departmental managers pick people already in their employment or who are known to them in the industry. However, these jobs are advertised too, but here it is proven experience rather than qualifications which is required.

Salary

No specific information can be given here as rates vary considerably from one laboratory to the next. However, as a general guide a good machine operator could earn a maximum of about £5,000–£6,000 a year, a technician about £6,000–£7,000 and a manager about £14,000–£17,000.

Case Study

Richard has been in the business for 22 years and now *manages* a very modern photofinishing laboratory.

> Originally, I trained to be a commercial artist. I soon realised that unless I was brilliant, which I wasn't, there would be few job prospects and a low salary.
>
> So I joined a photographic studio in London, originally as a general studio assistant. The studio carried on a general practice type of business. That is, portraits and weddings, but about 20 per cent of our work was commercial. Also associated with the studio was a photo-processing and finishing laboratory. A little later the studio side of the business was taken over, but I still carried on doing some wedding photography. However, as time went on I became more and more involved in the photofinishing side of the business. This was a very small colour department which had about eight staff.
>
> I had no formal training and mostly learnt as I went along. My first jobs were loading work ready to go on to the processors. Later, I started to process prints and then progressed to the really responsible work such as processing irreplaceable colour material.
>
> After that, I moved to another laboratory as production manager and then was promoted to laboratory manager. An opportunity came to move to a much bigger concern and I took it. Once again, I was first the production manager and then when the company changed hands I was promoted to laboratory manager. My last move a few years ago was within the company to head this laboratory situated in the Midlands.
>
> I see myself as among the last of a breed who came up through the business. I processed prints with my fingers and stained my finger nails with chemicals. In the early days you had to learn the hard way, and one person could have several responsibilities. This kind of opportunity is very rare today. Most labs like this one employ people to do a particular job and they become specialists, that is, they don't gain a general experience. They are very unlikely to move to management unless then are lucky enough to be picked and earmarked for that type of vocational 'grooming'.
>
> I wouldn't recommend starting at the bottom of the ladder in this job if you are looking for a career. The job is now so highly specialised and technical that increasingly the need is for highly numerate

people with computing skills. At least that is the way that the business seems to be going.

What is exciting about this business is that in a time of recession this is one area which is showing real growth. It's easy to introduce the new technology because there is the demand. For instance, we are operating with the same staff as ten years ago, but are handling four times as much work. I've just returned from a manufacturers' exhibition in Germany. The equipment and machinery which are becoming available are absolutely amazing. Photography is a growing market and it has never been cheaper.

Chapter 6

Professional Photofinishing Laboratories

Introduction

Professional photofinishing is showing some signs that it too will be following the trend towards increased automation. However, there is still considerable scope for the artisan and craftsman in this field. This is because there are many specialist processes which are best done by hand.

There is, at the present, a lack of skilled technicians in this trade. This too is a growing industry which can offer real career prospects. However, it is important that you realise that the employer is looking for someone who has a real interest in photofinishing. A failed photographer, who enters the trade because it is the next best thing, will often find the work mundane and perhaps frustrating. The industry needs dedicated specialists who are prepared to serve the needs of the professionial photographer. If a manager senses that you have chosen this career as a second option, you may be regarded as unsuitable. It is very important that you consider this point carefully.

One of the exciting aspects of working for a professional laboratory is that a school-leaver might join as a trainee, and eventually progress to the rank of laboratory manager. He would, of course, have to be prepared to move about the country and work in different laboratories to gain the necessary experience. If you proved yourself to be a highly skilled technician, say a hand colour printer or a retoucher, in the right laboratory you could earn quite a high salary.

Laboratories tend to specialise in either black and white or colour processes. If you began your training in colour work and then decided to move to monochrome, you might have to be prepared to start at the bottom again. If you want to avoid this possibility, you should decide early the type of photofinishing in which you are most interested.

No college at the moment offers a course which is really of any use to someone who wishes to begin in this side of the trade. Instead, many of the larger companies offer their own in-service training courses. It is best, therefore, to begin at a laboratory as a school-leaver with a good general and scientific education. You would then be taken on as a trainee and given very expert tuition which will best fit you for your occupation.

Some of the different specialist services provided by these laboratories are described in the following sections.

Processor

The processing of colour materials tends to be much more automated than for black and white. For colour processing, solution temperatures, concentrations and timing of each process are much more critical.

Initially you might be involved in recognising the different types of film and sorting them ready for processing. This may sound simple but it is a very important job. If the wrong type of film is put through a machine, this could contaminate the processing solutions resulting in damage to many hundreds of films. Besides black and white negative films, there are colour negative and transparency films (slides) which may be in 35mm, roll film or sheet form.

For processing, film can either be hung from racks which are dipped into the solutions (called dip and dunk), or lengths of film may be joined together and led through a system of rollers which feeds the film through each solution. This is known as continuous roll processing.

The machine and the chemical solutions have to be monitored very carefully. Each day before processing begins, the processor has to put test film through to check the machine's operation. These test films are often sent to the manufacturers of the chemicals and equipment, and are checked by specialists to ensure that everything is correct.

It is worth emphasising that this is a very responsible job. The processor is dealing with photographers' original material. One mistake could ruin thousands of pounds' worth of time, air fares, model fees and careful planning. This would result in a loss to the laboratory of vital custom and earn it a poor reputation.

Printer

Prints can either be made by hand or by using machines varying in degree of automation. Training to be expert in the former obviously takes longer and requires greater skill.

A colour printer naturally requires perfect colour vision. A negative is placed in the enlarger and light is shone through it and focused on to a base board where the printing paper is placed. The colour of the light being projected can be altered and adjusted very finely by three dials on the head of the enlarger. These dials move different coloured filters into the beam of light. The printer has to adjust the filtration and length of exposure to achieve the best possible print. An automatic machine printer controls many of these operations itself. However, the operator still has to judge the final result and decide if adjustments have to be made.

Internegative Maker

Sometimes prints are required from a colour transparency. The transparency must be rephotographed and the resulting negative is then used by the printer. Considerable skill is required by the technician to ensure correct filtration, and that the negative has recorded maximum detail from both highlight and shadow areas.

Duper

The duper makes exact copies of a transparency. Sometimes the duplicate has to be larger than the original. In all cases the procedure is basically the same. The original is rephotographed on to special duplicating film. In order that the original and duplicate are an exact match, great care must be taken to ensure sharp focus, filtration and exposure.

Copyist

A copyist uses a special camera to rephotograph artwork, text, illustrations and so on. The resulting copy photograph can then be used for printing purposes.

Photocomping

This is similar work to copying but here several images have to be combined on to a sheet of film. That is, a composite photograph is made from several separate images.

To do this, part of the film must be masked from the light while one image is projected on to the film. The mask is then changed and another image is projected until the required composite is achieved.

This is a highly skilled job and is often used in advertising to achieve special effects. 'Hard masks' may be laid directly on top of the film or a 'soft mask' may be separated from the film by transparent layers of varying thickness so that a soft edge effect is achieved.

Retouching

This is one of the most highly skilled and can also be one of the highest paid jobs. It requires considerable artistic skill and the ability to match colours exactly.

Prints are very often 'spotted' with a special pencil or with a fine paint brush. Coloured or black and white pigments are used to mask areas which may show blemishes from printing. For example, dust or hairs may have prevented light from reaching some areas of the print and these may have remained unexposed.

Even more skilled and responsible is the retouching of original material such as negatives or transparencies. Sometimes whole areas of a photograph may need to be removed or their colour changed. This is used a lot in advertising for the production of special effects. Entirely new images may be created by combining several images, and using airbrushes, paint brushes and cotton wool buds dipped in special pigments to make the final illusion quite convincing.

Dye Transfer

This is a highly expensive but top quality method of achieving a colour print from an original transparency. The transparency is projected through different filters and separation negatives are made. Further negatives are made which record highlight and shadow details. These are then projected on to separate sheets of matrix film. Once these are developed, they are dipped into a dye of a colour complementary to that of the original filter. Each dyed matrix is then pressed on to a sheet of special paper in turn until a full colour dye transfer print is produced.

Other Processes

Technicians may also be involved in the mounting of prints on to special boards or card for advertising and display. Prints may be covered and protected by a special plastic film. This process involves large presses and, depending on the exact procedure, may be known as encapsulation, heat sealing and so on. You may also be involved in the framing of photographs for display.

In a specialist photofinishing laboratory, there is not the same degree of specialisation as in wholesale photofinishing. You would be expected to have expertise in more than one skill. One day you might be working on a printing machine, then if the duper became ill you might do some of his work for a few days. This does mean that there can be quite a lot of variety, although there are many times when the work is purely routine.

Starting a Career

Jobs and openings for school-leavers are advertised in the trade press, such as the *British Journal of Photography*, photographic employment agencies and consultancies, and Jobcentres.

Salary

Rates vary greatly from one laboratory to another and depending on their location.

However, as a very general guide a trainee could expect to earn £3,000 per annum at the beginning. A qualified printer might earn about £8,000 and perhaps as much as £14,000 with overtime. A laboratory manager would earn at least £16,000–£25,000 per annum.

Case Study

Barry is manager of a large *specialist photofinishing laboratory*.

> I entered photography because I thought it would be exciting, interesting and different. At the time I began work in photography it had just started to appear 'respectable' because of the work of such people as Lord Snowdon, but I was much more a frustrated artist than a keen photographer.
>
> During my childhood I took very little interest in photography. I did at one stage buy a processing and contact printing set and enjoyed for

a time making prints in a large wardrobe, but the phase passed. My family had all been artists, art teachers or musicians and although I very much wanted to make pictures, the problem was I couldn't draw.

At school I had good teachers and worked hard, I don't think I was particularly able but eventually left school with six O levels.

My first job was a 'trainee hospital administrator'. I found this rather a strange job, sometimes interesting but often very boring. After three years I answered an advertisement for a general assistant in a general practice studio. Although I only had a few 35mm transparencies to show, I was given the job. It wasn't a thriving business but during the next three years I did a wide variety of photography, mostly weddings, babies, dances, Christmas grottos, shop fronts and some stage shots. The business also began to offer one of the first overnight processing services. We had to work very hard but it introduced me to d and p (developing and processing).

Shortly after, I moved to a larger town and began working for a very old, established laboratory. Their methods were very old fashioned, the results beautiful but all in all rather inefficient. However, I benefited enormously by learning the secrets of the craft from some very old members of staff who were near retirement.

I began to assist two of the staff photographers on location which contributed greatly to my enjoyment while I worked there. However, I noticed the colour work produced by another laboratory which was a competitor, in fact the same company that I now work for, and thought it was unbelievably good. I decided to write to them and shortly afterwards they took me on.

At first I was miserable! There was so much work to do and so much responsibility. I was insufficiently trained or experienced for the job I was doing and felt under great pressure. I kept working as hard as I could and gradually things got better and I was promoted to senior printer.

After three years I knew I would have to move to gain more experience. Out of curiosity more than anything, I applied to a photographic staff employment agency and obtained the job of staff consultant. During my stay I was never sure if I was a social worker/ careers officer or a slick salesman. The work was demanding, interesting, often amusing but I never really felt satisfied. I became involved at the same time with a very large and successful photographic studio in London, and helped them to set up and organise a colour processing line. This began to give me an insight into the workings of the top end of the market.

Eventually, because of my involvement with finding other people jobs I found one for myself. I became the manager of a colour processing laboratory. It was extremely hard work. In order to compete with other laboratories in the city, we sometimes had to work 12 hours a day. However, because of the way the company was set up I didn't have the freedom to organise things the way I wanted so I began to look for another job.

I rejoined the company, whose colour work I had so admired, as an area technical representative. My main responsibility was to ensure good communication between the laboratories' production staff and clients. I also found a lot of new business for the company.

At this time, many new laboratories were opening and there was an increasing demand for processing. I persuaded the company that a new laboratory was needed to handle the increased business and maintain our position against other competing laboratories. The company decided to go ahead and open a new laboratory and I was appointed manager.

At the present time, the laboratory is doing very well. When I look back on my career to date, I realise that I reached my position by showing reasonable skill, but more importantly by having a commitment to the company I chose to work for.

I received no formal training at any stage other than that given by my company at its head office. I have been lucky to work with some very competent people, and I have gained a lot of know-how through this sort of experience. After virtually a life-time in photography I still think it is different, exciting and interesting. The people in it tend to be friendly as a whole, and there is still a sort of amateurish enthusiasm in the business, probably not found in many others.

Promotion is most commonly awarded in the business because of merit. To gain promotion you have to be prepared to move jobs because very often the unit you work for has only limited opportunities. My career prospects at the moment are pretty static and will depend very much on the success that this laboratory enjoys.

Chapter 7

The Photographic Manufacturing, Retailing and Servicing Trades

Manufacturing

There is very little manufacture of cameras in the UK. Most of the major manufacturers are in Japan. Kodak and Polaroid do some manufacture in this country, but job opportunities are mainly limited to assembly and production line work. Most of the research and development goes on in the USA, but there are opportunities in companies involved in the importation, distribution and servicing of these products.

However, a considerable amount of software and photofinishing material is produced in the UK. This includes film, photographic papers and chemicals. Two of the major companies are Kodak, which employs about 6,000 staff and Ilford, now merged with Ciba-Geigy Ltd, which employs more than 2,000 staff.

These industries rely heavily on scientists and technicians. Between them, they are involved in a broad spectrum of related products: film, television, magnetic tape, computers and space technology as well as photographic materials.

Starting a Career

Production trainee schemes are run to train future supervisors and senior operators for the various departments. Entrants for the trainee schemes need to be 16 years of age or over and may have to sit a selection test. Much of the production machinery is highly automated and has to be maintained and serviced by engineers. There is also a need for printers, processors and quality controllers who do the same sorts of jobs as others in the photofinishing industry.

Phototechnicians

This field requires graduates in particular. Many will have higher degrees, most of them will be chemists, but some will also be physicists, engineers, computer scientists and others. The work involves the researching and developing of new products, the finding of new ways of ensuring that production and processing is being done most efficiently and economically. However, not only must these people be good in their specialised field, they must also be able to work as part of a team and be able to communicate information and ideas. This is because much of their time will be spent working with others on particular projects, developing new dyes, light sensitive coatings, or improving drying, cutting and packaging processes.

Laboratory Technicians and Assistants

Generally, you will be involved in assisting a senior colleague or analysing and testing film and processing. For this work, you need to have a considerable interest in science and be able to approach and solve problems methodically. You will be expected to attend day release courses to Higher National Certificate and even degree level.

Engineers

There is a requirement for a great variety of engineering skills. This includes electrical, mechanical, production and chemical engineers. You will mostly be involved on the production lines ensuring that everything to do with coatings, processing or manufacture will work consistently, reliably and predictably.

Graduate Engineers

Their role is usually supervisory, or else they work as 'trouble-shooters' having to solve production, processing and other problems quickly and efficiently. People with these skills are always in high demand and enjoy good employment prospects and salaries. Because so much of their work is highly specialised in nature they also receive in-house training.

There are also a large number of other skilled occupations. Technician engineers provide technical back-up for the craft personnel. This could involve the maintenance of ventilation and other systems. Often a large number of craftsmen are employed, from bricklayers to fitters and metal workers. Some apprenticeships are offered in these trades. Machine operators perform a similar role to those in wholesale photofinishing. Their work is highly specialised, and they often receive in-house training to operate machines either involved in processing or production of photographic materials.

Marketing Staff

Sometimes graduate trainees are recruited. However, there are also openings for people with marketing experience, even in other fields. This is an extremely skilled and responsible job. You must be able to analyse the needs and demands for your company's products. This will involve close liaison both with the buyers of your products and your company's representatives and production staff.

If you are a graduate and wish to find out more information about employment you should consult a copy of the *Directory of Opportunities for Graduates*, published by Newpoint Ltd, 76 St James's Lane, London N10 3RD.

Salary

Operators and processors are usually paid hourly and work on average a 37½ hour week. Their wages total about £8,500 per annum. Initially they start at about £6,500 per annum as a handler or machine assistant.

A non-graduate of about 18 years of age, with ONC or two A levels, could expect to start on a salary of about £6,400 per year. Salaries progress more slowly for non-graduates, and reach an average of about £10,000 per annum after about 10 years. After that, it would be necessary to gain higher qualifications in order to attain more senior positions.

Many graduates are recruited in the September/October 'milkrun' or according to demand. A science graduate can expect a starting salary of about £9,500 per annum. A graduate who is good at his job can expect to reach a high salary level depending on ability and rate of promotion, with an average of about £20,000 per year. This is usually attained around 35 years of age.

The Retail Trade

Photographic equipment is sold through all sorts of shops, specialist, general, large and small. If you have mostly a hobby interest in photography, you may find it possible to work as a sales assistant in a small retail shop. In the larger discount retailers a college education may be beneficial. If you wish to make a career of photographic retailing, you should ask during interview whether the company provides courses and in-house training and what it involves.

No matter where you work, you will have to provide a service which differs only in the degree of specialist knowledge required. You need a good general understanding of photographic equipment and principles. Often you will be faced with a customer who is not at all sure what he requires, be it camera or film. You must be able to question him carefully, so that you can suggest equipment which is best suited to his needs, experience and wallet. You may also be asked to examine customers' photographs and explain what has gone wrong.

As stated previously, photography is a growing but competitive market. At present, there are many opportunities within the retail trade, and it enjoys good job security.

At the moment there is no representative organisation for the trade.

Repairs and Servicing

Modern photographic equipment is highly automated and owes much to electronics. Trainees need, therefore, a good knowledge of photography and science, physics and electronics in particular. Because so much equipment these days is highly specialised, the majority of your training would be in-house and conducted by a particular photographic importer or distributor. You can contact the representative organisation, the Institute of Photographic Repair Technicians (IPART), for further information.

IPART is the trade organisation for the photographic repair industry. Membership is conferred only after the association's conditions and standards are met and bestows a high status on individuals or organisations admitted. It will act as an arbiter in disputes between customer and repairer and provides a forum for discussion within the trade.

Part 2

Chapter 8

Courses Available

There is a vast number of part-time, full-time, independent and specialist, and correspondence courses available. Some lead to degrees, diplomas, certificates and other awards. In fact, the variety could be bewildering for someone who is looking for a recommended and appropriate form of training. If you are in any doubt, you would be well advised to contact the professional associations which represent those areas of photography in which you are most interested. They will be prepared to indicate which courses are best to meet your needs and how you can obtain further information. The addresses of professional associations are listed in 'Useful Addresses' (see p 90).

You would be well advised to try to get as broad an idea as possible of the market for photographs. This is to make sure that the course you choose will fit you for an occupation where there is actually a need for photographers. Course content and emphasis vary considerably. Some tend to specialise and others cover a variety of fields. The following lists include only courses which are predominantly devoted to photography. Where the course has a definite emphasis, or is biased towards preparing the student for a particular type of photography, this will be indicated.

You should also remember that many companies who provide specialist photographic or laboratory services have their own training schemes. You should, therefore, consider all these factors carefully before committing yourself to a particular course of training.

City and Guilds or Equivalent Courses

Entry qualifications usually demand that the applicant is already employed or has been promised employment in photography. To enter for a course, you should have gained at least two

O level/GCSE passes including English; some courses require A levels. There are two main schemes, 744 general photography and 745 scientific and technical photography.

The general photography scheme is intended for those who are employed as photographers, studio assistants or printers in the fields of portraiture, commercial, advertising and fashion photography and in photojournalism.

The scientific and technical photography scheme is more suited to those who are employed in photography and as technical staff in industry, hospitals, research and allied fields. Both schemes have been devised on the assumption that normally students will attend a college on a part-time day or block release basis from work in the photographic industry; they are intended to complement the training and experience which the student will obtain in his employment. The syllabuses will cover the following topics.

744 General Photography
Cameras, monochrome photography, colour photography, lighting, the darkroom, visual aids and graphic reproduction, organisation and administration, safety, application, design, reproduction of photographs, audio-visual aids, administration, business methods, photography in the service of advertising and commerce.

745 Scientific and Technical Photography
Cameras, monochrome photography, colour photography, lighting, the darkroom, visual aids and graphic reproduction, organisation and administration, safety, applications, science, tone reproduction, audio-visual aids, administration, photography in the service of research and industry.

Each of these courses is also available at an advanced level. The advanced level courses cover the same syllabus but in greater depth. To enter for such a course you need to have a City and Guilds certificate at the lower level or an equivalent qualification.

Ashton under Lyne
Tameside College of Technology, Beaufort Road, Ashton under Lyne, Lancashire OL6 6NX; 061-330 6991
744, 3 years, day release

Birmingham
City of Birmingham Polytechnic, Faculty of Art and Design, Gosta Green, Birmingham B4 7DX; 021-359 6721 ext 237

744, 3 years, day release and evening

Croydon
Croydon College School of Design and Technology, Fairfield, Croydon CR9 1DX; 01-688 9271
744, 2 years, day release

Dagenham
Barking College of Technology, Charlecote Road, Dagenham, Essex RM8 3LD; 01-579 2217
744 and 745, 3 years, day release; advanced 744 and 745, 2 years, day release
Also specialist short course of 20 weeks: (a) advanced studio techniques, (b) colour printing, (c) technical applications

Derby
Derbyshire College of Higher Education, Kedleston Road, Derby DE3 5GX; 03321 47181 ext 36
744, 3 years, day release; advanced 744, 3 years, day release

Edinburgh
Napier College of Commerce and Technology, Department of Photography, 61 Marchmont Road, Edinburgh EH9 1HU; 031-444 2266
4 years, day release or evening
SCOTVEC higher and ordinary certificates in photography

Ewell
North East Surrey College of Technology, Reigate Road, Ewell, Epsom, Surrey KT17 3DS; 03727 1731 ext 240 (from London 01-394 1731)
744 and 745, day release and evening
Special level evening course in general photographic techniques, 1-3 years
BIPP basic certificate in medical photography, unspecified duration, day release
NESCOT diploma in colour processing, 1 year, evening

Glasgow
Glasgow College of Building and Printing, Department of Photography and Graphics, 60 North Hanover Street, Glasgow G1 2BP; 041-332 9969 ext 268
744, 3 years, day release; 745, 2 years, day release; advanced 744 and 745, 5 years, day release
SCOTVEC 810 photography/audio-visual certificate, 2 years, day release, higher certificate, 4 years day release
Medical photography (IMBI modules), 2 years, day release and evening
Advanced colour techniques, 1 year, evening

Gloucester
Gloucestershire College of Arts and Technology, Oxstalls Lane, Gloucester GL2 9HW; 0452 26321
744 and 745, 3 years, day release
This college liaises with the AFAEP

Halesowen
Halesowen College of Further Education, Whittingham Road, Halesowen B63 3NA; 021550 1451/2477
Colour printing, 8 weeks, evening

Huntingdon
Huntingdon Technical College, California Road, Huntingdon, Cambridgeshire PE18 7BL; 0480 52346
744, 2 years, day release

Leeds
Kitson College of Technology, Cookridge Street, Leeds, West Yorkshire LS2 8BL; 0532 430381
744 and 745, 3 years, day release; advanced 744 and 745, 2 years, day release
Colour photography, 1 year, evening
Photomicrography, 10 weeks, evening
Photography in audio-visual aids, 10 weeks, evening or half day, day release
Applied photographic techniques for research and industry, 8 weeks, half day, day release

Leicester
South Fields College of Further Education, Aylestone Road, Leicester LE2 7LW; 0533 541818
744

Liverpool
Central Liverpool College of Further Education, Department of Printing, Design and Photography, Hope Street, Liverpool, Merseyside L1 9EB; 051-708 0432 ext 31
744, 3 years, day release; advanced 744, two years, day release

London
Paddington College, University of London, Paddington Green, London W2 1NB; 01-402 6221 ext 48
744 and 745, 3 years, day release/evening; advanced 744 and 745, 2 years, day release/evening
Holography - special course

Norwich
Norwich City College of Further and Higher Education, Ipswich Road, Norwich NR2 2LJ; 0603 60011
Special course on medical and forensic studies, 1 term, day release

Nottingham
South Nottinghamshire College of Further Education, Greythorn Drive, West Bridgford, Nottingham NG2 7GA; 0602 812125
744, 2 years, full-time, day release college diploma

Nuneaton
North Warwickshire College of Technology and Art, Hinckley Road, Nuneaton, Warwickshire CV11 6BH; 0203 349321
744, 2 years, evening

Oxford
Oxford College of Further Education, Oxpens Road, Oxford OX1 1SA; 0865 245871
Techniques, aesthetics and philosophy of monochrome photography, 20 weeks, evening

Plymouth
Plymouth College of Art and Design, Tavistock Place, Plymouth, Devon PL4 8AT; 0752 21312
Advanced 744, 1 year, full-time

Portsmouth
Portsmouth College of Art, Design and Further Education, Winston Churchill Avenue, Portsmouth, Hampshire PO1 2DJ; 0705 753366
Basic photography, 10 weeks; studio techniques, 8 weeks, evening; portraiture, 6 weeks, evening; colour printing, 7 weeks, evening

Reading
Berkshire College of Art and Design, Kings Road, Reading, Berkshire RG1 4HJ; 0734 583501
744 and 845, 3 years, day release; advanced 744 and 745, 2 years, day release
Commercial technical and scientific courses for those already in photographic employment

Rumney
Rumney College of Technology, Trowbridge Road, Rumney, Cardiff CF3 8XZ; 0222 794226 ext 12
744, 3 years, day release

St Albans
Hertfordshire College of Art and Design, 7 Hatfield Road, St Albans, Hertfordshire AL1 3RS; 0727 6441
On-going workshop for practising teachers, on a technical consultancy basis, evening

Salisbury
Salisbury College of Art, Southampton Road, Salisbury, Wiltshire SP1 2LW; 0722 23711
745, day release and evening; advanced 745, day release and evening

Sheffield
Granville College, Department of Art and Design, Granville Road, Sheffield, South Yorkshire S2 2RL; 0742 760271
BTEC certificate, 2 years, day release

Swansea
West Glamorgan Institute of Higher Education, Faculty of Art and Design, Townhill Campus, Townhill Road, Swansea, West Glamorgan SA2 0UT; 0792 23482
BTEC diploma course

Twickenham
Richmond-upon-Thames College, Egerton Road, Twickenham TW2 7SJ; 01-892 6656
744, 3 years, day release; 745, 2 years, day release; advanced 745, 3 years, day release
BTEC certificate/diploma, 3 years, day release
Advanced colour photography course, 1 year, evening BIPP vocational diploma, 3 years, day release

Ware
Ware College, Department of Design and Distribution, Scotts Road, Ware, Hertfordshire SG12 9JF; 0920 5441
744, 3 years, day release

Wednesbury
West Bromwich College of Commerce and Technology, Department of Photography, Kendrick Street, Wednesbury, West Midlands WS10 0PE; 021-569 4592
845, 3 years, day release

College Diploma and Certificate Courses

Course contents and emphasis vary considerably. If you wish to gain a comprehensive idea of the full range of institutions which offer courses, these can be found in *The British Journal Directory of Photographic Education*. Full details of this publication can be found on p 92. You will probably find that your local library will have a copy, but make sure that it is the latest edition as the situation can change from year to year.

Courses usually last from two to three years. Some are biased towards those who are already employed in some field of photography, while others are only meant to give a broad view of the subject.

Entry requirements vary depending on the course and the institution. Some of the two-year courses require a standard of education varying from CSE grade 2 to O levels in three or four subjects. Others specify a minimum of five O levels including English. The latter standard applies to most of the three-year courses, preferably including English language, maths and physics. Photography O and A levels are also acceptable to most colleges. GCSEs will apply from summer 1988.

Some of the colleges have cooperated over a number of years with the various professional photographic associations. The British Institute of Professional Photography (BIPP) has been particularly notable in this respect and has established, in conjunction with a number of colleges, courses specifically geared to the needs of the professional. The Association of Fashion, Advertising and Professional Photographers (AFAEP) is also working closely with a number of colleges. More details can be obtained by contacting the relevant associations.

Examinations validated by the BIPP are held at two levels. Two-year full-time and three-year part-time courses lead to the vocational examination. Three-year full-time (or the appropriate part-time) courses lead to the professional qualifying examination. The BIPP also organises its own examinations in the field of medical photography. More details of this are included in a later section. Advanced courses recognised by the BIPP and HND higher courses do qualify for mandatory awards.

The Professional Qualifying Examination

The educational requirements for admission to the following courses are five passes at GCSE level (or equivalent) including English language, and at least two subjects at A level.

*These colleges liaise with the AFAEP.

Blackpool and Fylde College,* Department of Photography, Palatine Road, Blackpool FY1 4DW; 0253 293071 ext 47
Course emphasises the creative and analytical approach in dealing with advertising, industrial, and general practice professional photography, 3 years, full-time

Dorset College of Further Education,* Department of Visual Communication, Main College Building, Lansdowne, Bournemouth, Dorset BH1 3JI; 0202 20772
Photography and film, with emphasis on advertising, fashion and editorial photography, 3 years, full-time

Harrow College of Higher Education,* Northwick Park, Harrow HA1 3TP; 01-864 5422
Applied photography, film and television, part-time/full-time

Polytechnic of Central London, 18–22 Riding House Street, London W1 7PD; 01-486 5811 ext 6445
A broad-based course in professional photography, 4 years, part-time

Salisbury College of Art,* Southampton Road, Salisbury, Wiltshire SP1 2LW; 0722 23711
General photography for industry and commerce, 3 years, full-time

The Vocational Examination

The educational requirements for admission to the following courses are four GCSEs (or equivalent) in English language, maths, or a science subject, an arts subject and one other.

Full-time Courses of Two Years' Duration Recognised and Validated by the BIPP
Napier College of Commerce and Technology, 219 Colinton Road, Edinburgh EH14 1DJ; 031-444 2266

Glasgow College of Building and Printing, 60 North Hanover Street, Glasgow G1 1BP; 041-332 9969 ext 268

Kitson College of Technology, Cookridge Street, Leeds LS2 8BL; 0532 430381

Plymouth College of Art and Design, Tavistock Place, Plymouth PL4 8AT; 0752 21312

Berkshire College of Art and Design, Kings Road, Reading RG1 4HJ; 0743 583501

Sandwell College of Further and Higher Education, Department of Photography, Kendrick Street, Wednesbury, West Midlands WS10 9ER; 021-569 4592

Three-year Part-time Courses Recognised and Validated by the BIPP
Richmond-upon-Thames College, Egerton Road, Twickenham TW2 7SJ; 01-892 6656

BTEC and SCOTVEC

The validating organisations for photographic training courses are the Business and Technician Education Council (BTEC), and the Scottish Vocational Education Council (SCOTVEC). Colleges may submit their own syllabuses to BTEC for examination. If the organisation validates the course, this indicates that it comes up to their standard. However, this implies no uniformity of course content, only standard. You will, therefore, have to examine any such syllabus carefully to ensure that it corresponds to your needs and interests.

The situation with SCOTVEC, on the other hand, is different. Here the syllabuses conform to a nationally agreed policy and to a national minimum standard. Further information is available from SCOTVEC (see p 91).

Degree Courses

There is currently no degree course in photography offered by a British university. However, a number of other institutions do offer photography courses up to first degree level. There are three degree courses which have been approved by the BIPP. These are listed below together with a number of other major courses. The award is made by the Council for National Academic Awards (CNAA).

Application for most of these courses should be made either to the Art and Design Admissions Registry (ADAR) or the Polytechnic Central Admissions System (PCAS), at the beginning of February for courses commencing that autumn. The relevant body for applications is indicated after the course details. You should nominate your first and second choices of institution and return your form by the end of March.

Applicants must be at least 18 years of age and possess qualifications as laid down by the CNAA for art and design courses. This is normally:

Five GCE passes, two of which must be A level, or
Five O level passes and 1-year art and design foundation course successfully completed, or
Four GCE passes, one of which is at A level, and successful completion of 1-year art and design foundation course, or
In exceptional circumstances other qualifications may be acceptable to the CNAA.

NB For exact entry requirements you are advised to contact the institution concerned.

Derbyshire College of Higher Education, Kedleston Road, Derby DE3 5GX; 03321 47181
BA (Hons) Creative Photography - ADAR

Harrow College of Higher Education (see p 76)
BA (Hons) in Applied Photography, Film and Television - ADAR

London College of Printing, Elephant and Castle, London SE1 6SB; 01-735 8484/9100

BA (Hons) Visual Communication (Photography/Film/Television) - ADAR

Manchester Polytechnic, Department of Communication, Art and Design, Chatham Building, All Saints, Manchester M15 6BR; 061-228 6171
BA (Hons) Design for Communication Media
Course offers specialisation in (a) photographic studies, or (b) film and television studies - PCAS

Napier College of Commerce and Technology, Colinton Road, Edinburgh EH10 5DT; 031-447 7070
BA (Hons) Photographic
Essentially a practical course designed to prepare the graduate to enter the professional photography and audio-visual media - ADAR

Polytechnic of Central London* (see p 77)
1. BA (Hons) in Film and Photographic Arts
2. BSc (Hons) in Photographic Sciences - PCAS

Trent Polytechnic,* School of Art and Design, Bonington Building, Dryden Street, Nottingham NG1 4FZ; 0602 48248 ext 2516
BA (Hons) Photography.
Broad education in creative applications of still photography based on understanding of its technique and history - PCAS

West Surrey College of Art and Design, Falkner Road, The Hart, Farnham, Surrey GU9 7DS
BA (Hons) Photography, Film and Video, Animation
Essentially a practical course, emphasising exploration and experimentation, and development of creative and conceptual understanding - ADAR

*These colleges liaise with the AFAEP.

Postgraduate Courses

There is a wide variety of courses available. (See also *The British Journal Directory of Photographic Education.*)

MA COURSE

Manchester Polytechnic, Department of Communication, Art and Design, Chatham Building, All Saints, Manchester M15 6BR; 061-228 6171 ext 2265
Offers opportunity for students to explore areas and topics of their own special interest. Apply through ADAR. 4 terms full-time, 7 terms part-time.

Royal College of Art, Department of Photography, 23 Cromwell Road, London SW7; 01-584 5020 ext 286

Photography (RCA), development of individual's original vision as well as technical photographic skills

'Lens Media' in Teacher Training and Educational Technology Courses
King Alfred's College, Sparkford Road, Winchester, Hampshire SO22 4NR; 0962 62281 ext 204
Photography in schools: certificate in further professional studies, designed to extend the capabilities and interest of teachers in photography as a subject and teaching tool. Apply direct to college, 2 terms, part-time and evening

Worcester College of Higher Education, Henwick Grove, Worcester WR2 6AJ; 0905 428080 ext 206
Certificate in photography and printmaking. General course to develop skills. Time available to prepare teaching material and make equipment suitable for school use

Specialist Courses

MEDICAL PHOTOGRAPHY

For information on courses for trainees write to:

The School of Medical Photography, South Glamorgan Area Health Authority, University Hospital of Wales, Heath Park, Cardiff

The Secretary, London School of Medical Photography, c/o Institute of Dermatology, St John's Hospital, 5 Lisle Street, London WC2

Information on the BIPP/IMBI examinations in medical photography can be obtained by writing to the education and training officer of the BIPP, or by contacting the Secretary, IMBI.

Press Photography

A one-year full-time course for potential press photographers is being held at the Richmond College of Further Education, Sheffield. Local education authorities may award grants. You would be expected to live locally in lodgings. If you are interested in the course you should enquire early to your LEA.

To be selected for the course, candidates suitable for consideration will be asked to attend initially at regional centres for a day of aptitude tests. Those who pass these tests will be invited on another day for interviews with panels including experienced people from the industry. Applicants are expected to meet their own expenses if invited to attend for these tests or interviews.

The deadline for applications is the 31st March, but forms should be returned before this date. Applications and further details are available from the National Council for the Training of Journalists (NCTJ). Make sure that you enclose a stamped, self-addressed envelope with all correspondence. General career information may also be obtained by writing to the Training Department, Newspaper Society (see p 91).

Private Courses

There is a large number of such courses - the best known is given below.

The Photographer's Place, Bradbourne, Ashbourne, Derbyshire
DE6 1PB; 033 525 392
All aspects of photography. Short courses, workshops, seminars, etc.

Chapter 9

Entry to Courses

Introduction

In the preceding sections it has been attempted where possible to give an indication of the sorts of minimum educational qualifications required for entry to a course. However, of the many potential entrants to any course, only some will be selected from the short list after interview. Indeed, your performance in the interview can be even more important than your educational qualifications.

Very often the interview will be conducted by several people making up an interview panel. They are there to ensure that you are the right person for their course and will gain maximum benefit from it. Whether the course is one intended to train a potential professional photographer or is more academically oriented, the panel will in general be looking for the same attributes in the interviewee:

1. Has he/she an enquiring mind?
2. Has he/she got a sincere interest in photography?
3. Has he/she the stamina to 'stay the course' despite frustrations and occasional set-backs?
4. Does photography play much of a part in his/her spectrum of wider interests?
5. Can he/she communicate ideas in conversation and on paper?

One of the most important things to do, therefore, long before applications and interviews, is to ensure that you have chosen the right institution and the right course. To do this, you will need to look as carefully as possible at the different types of photographic career on offer. Assuming that you have decided what is right for you, you should list those courses which appeal most. Then you should contact those institutions and try to find out more. Even better, try to visit the institution. Try to go when the students have an exhibition of their work. Try to find out what sorts of equipment and facilities are available. You may also be able to obtain at least some idea what the staff and technicians are like. Find out if any of the staff have any real experience in the field of photography which most interests you. Find out if the tutors have any active contact with relevant professional organisations. From this you should be able to get a fairly clear idea of the course's standards and specialisations.

To do all this it is a good idea to start at least a year in advance.

At many interviews, you will be expected to show examples of your work, that is, a portfolio. Make sure that your portfolio is neat, representative, and well presented. The panel will take your portfolio as a major indicator of your taste, talents, and compatibility with the course.

Awards and Finance

As soon as you know that you have been offered a place on a course, you should contact the awards section of your local education authority. Some courses warrant a mandatory and others a discretionary grant award. That is, you may not necessarily get a grant for some courses even if you have been offered a place. If grant aid is an important factor in your further education, this is something which you ought to consider when initially choosing a course. More details can be found in the booklet 'Grants to Students: a Brief Guide', which can be obtained from the LEA or Department of Education and Science.

Students from EEC countries pay the same fees as UK students and will receive grant aid from their own country. Overseas students must meet their own course fees which are not subsidised. There are no grants, funds or trusts available in this country to pay for your tuition. You must make sure of your own funding before leaving your home country.

If you have to meet some or all of your course fees, you will have to prove that you can maintain yourself financially for the entire duration of your course. Self-financing students should also be aware that on many courses registration fees are payable. For instance, CNAA registration for the academic year 1987/88 is £50.

You should also bear in mind that all fees may rise from year to year and that you will have to meet transport and all other living expenses. You may even have to pay something towards the cost of materials for your course, even if you have received a grant from your LEA. As of 1986, LEA equipment grants have been abolished. You would need, therefore, to meet the cost of many materials and equipment from your own resources.

Chapter 10

Representative Organisations and Professional Associations

Introduction

There are organisations and associations which represent virtually every field of photography. All are funded by fees paid by their members. Each is, therefore, very concerned to ensure that their members get good value for money. There is some variation in the exact nature of the services they offer their membership. However, most are concerned to give advice to those seeking entry to the profession, and many are involved in vocational training and photographic education. Some provide information to their members about developments in the field, provide newsletters or magazines, organise meetings and seminars and so on. Membership of some associations can provide some prestige. In others, membership is according to a hierarchy based on your experience and ability. It is also true to say that some clients may feel more confident in approaching a photographer whose record of membership shows he is competent and reliable.

The Arts Council of Great Britain

The council is involved in the stimulation and development of photography. It can help and advise on careers and training. It offers grants to support photographic research and critical writing.

It will also help with advice and subsidies for exhibitions by independent organisations. For specific advice and enquiries write to the photography officer of the council.

The Association of Fashion, Advertising and Editorial Photographers (AFAEP)

To become a member, one has first to be proposed and seconded by persons who are already members. You must be able to prove that you are an established photographer working in a field of photography. This proof is usually furnished in the form of portfolio of work appropriate to the association. Many of the most well-respected British photographers belong to this association.

The association keeps a register of individuals who can offer services to photographers. For example, stylists, accessorisers, etc. It will also provide advice on professional problems, offer legal or ethical advice, or will negotiate on behalf of the membership. It may also give advice on careers and training and be actively involved with a number of training colleges. Until recently the Association provided a career workshop on Thursdays at 3 pm for 45 minutes. These proved so popular and useful that they are likely to be restarted in the near future.

British Association of Picture Libraries and Agencies (BAPLA)

Established to allow communication within the trade and to provide a united voice to negotiate fees, agree policies and provide benefits. BAPLA publishes a newsletter providing information to the membership and keeps a register of the holdings of its member agencies and libraries.

British Institute of Professional Photography (BIPP)

The BIPP is a qualifying organisation for UK members. It recognises over 30 different photographic specialisations.

It represents professional photographers' interests in connection with the law and society. It will also discipline members whom it feels have behaved unprofessionally. The BIPP also organises conferences, exhibitions, seminars and workshops for its members.

Membership is organised on a hierarchial basis. There are five non-corporate grades of membership: student member, graduate, junior photographic technician, affiliated and retired members.

Corporate membership demands a high standard of photographic skill. It is achieved either by examination or by the submission of a portfolio which shows a sufficient degree of competence in the field. Corporate membership is at three levels: licentiate, associate, and fellowship. All applicants for membership must certify that they are full-time professional photographers. The Institute publishes a journal, *The Photographer*.

Bureau of Freelance Photographers (BFP)

The BFP stipulates no minimum standard for membership. Services include a monthly newsletter indicating the editorial photographic requirement of a wide range of publications. This can be very useful to the freelance and keeps him in touch with trends and markets. The BFP also operates an advisory service to help members with queries and problems. Proof of membership will enable you to receive discount on goods purchased from some retailers. The BFP publish a list of such retailers.

Chartered Society of Designers

Membership includes photographers and teachers of photography.

Confederation of Photographic Industries (CPI)

As the name implies this is an umbrella organisation which includes many other member organisations such as the BIPP, MPA and others representing photographic manufacture, import, retailing and processing laboratories. The organisation seeks to promote communication between the different sectors of the industry and to provide a united voice on its behalf.

The Institute of Medical and Biological Illustration (IMBI)

The IMBI was founded in 1968 as a professional body for all those engaged in audiovisual communication in the life sciences.

The institute offers membership to artists, photographers, and audio-visual personnel working in medicine, biology, agriculture, botany, veterinary science and zoology.

The IMBI provides its own qualifying examination and works in conjunction with the BIPP. The institute holds an annual conference for its members and produces a variety of publications. It also advises unions and official bodies on matters relating to career structure and salary scales.

Master Photographers' Association (MPA)

Membership is only open to full-time professional photographers. You can either apply for membership by submitting references for ordinary membership, or by providing a satisfactory portfolio of work. After six months, you can apply for associate membership by providing a satisfactory sample of 20 pieces of work. After three years, you can apply for fellowship but you must provide evidence of service to the profession and the community.

The MPA offers its members special insurance rates and arranges seminars and training courses, as well as providing legal and accounting advice. As an affiliated member of the Federation of European Photographers it can advise members travelling overseas and even arrange accommodation and contacts at their proposed destination. It publishes a monthly magazine called *Master Photographer*.

Royal Photographic Society (RPS)

The RPS was founded in 1853. It seeks to represent and stimulate all areas of photography. There are a number of special interest groups for members and they arrange lectures, seminars, exhibitions and workshops.

Membership is hierarchical: licentiate, associate and fellow of the RPS. Work is submitted to the appropriate panel for assessment. Exemption from having to initially become a licentiate can be given if you hold certain recognised qualifications.

The RPS National Centre of Photography, houses a permanent exhibition, lecture theatre and cinema, and the RPS collections

Society of Picture Researchers and Editors (SPREd)

The society provides legal advice, guidance, training and can occasionally advise on career opportunities. It aims to act as a voice for the profession, to promote its interests, and to enable members to exchange ideas and experiences.

Chapter 11

Unions

Employees and freelances can play such a variety of roles within the photographic trade that a large number of unions are involved. In certain trades, associated with the press side of the business, you may be obliged to join a union if you are to be employed. However, there are also a great many trades where union membership is left to the discretion of the individual.

It is not a subject over which you should become unduly anxious. When you make enquiries about following a particular career, you will be able to find out the situation as regards union membership.

Following is a list of some of the appropriate unions for workers within the field of photography.

ABS	Association of Broadcasting Staff
ACTT	Association of Cinematographic, Television and Allied Technicians
ASTMS	Association of Scientific, Technical and Managerial Staff
AUEW	Amalgamated Union of Engineering Workers (TAS section)
IOJ	Institute of Journalists (not affiliated to the TUC)
IPCS	Institution of Professional Civil Servants
NALGO	National Association of Local Government Officers
NATSOPA	National Society of Operative Printers and Assistants
NGA	National Graphical Association
NUJ	National Union of Journalists (editorial and press photography)
SLADE	Society of Lithographic Artists, Designers and Engravers
SOGAT	Society of Graphical and Allied Trades
TGWU	Trades and General Workers' Union
USDAW	Union of Shop, Distributive and Allied Workers

Chapter 12

Useful Addresses and Journals

Useful Addresses

Art and Design Admissions Registry
9 Broad Street, Hereford HR4 9AP

Arts Council of Great Britain
105 Piccadilly, London W1V 0AU; 01-629 9495

Association of Fashion, Advertising and Editorial Photographers (AFAEP), 9 Domingo Street, London EC1Y 0TA

British Association of Picture Libraries and Agencies (BAPLA)
c/o PO Box 284, London W11 4RP

British Institute of Professional Photography (BIPP)
2 Amwell End, Ware, Hertfordshire SG12 9HN; 0920 4011

Business and Technician Education Council (BTEC)
Central House, Upper Woburn Street, London WC1H 0HE;
01-388 3288

Chartered Society of Designers
29 Bedford Square, London WC1B 2ED; 01-631 1510

City and Guilds of London Institute
46 Britannia Street, London WC1X 9RG; 01-278 2468

Civil Service Commission
Alencon Link, Basingstoke, Hampshire RG21 1JB; 0256 29222

Council for National Academic Awards
344-354 Gray's Inn Road, London WC1X 8BP; 01-278 4411

Department of Education and Science
Elizabeth House, York Road, London SE1 7PH; 01-934 9000

The Institute of Medical and Biological Illustrators (IMBI)
27 Craven Street, London WC2N 5NX

Institute of Photographic Apparatus Repair Technicians (IPART)
228 Regents Park Road, London N3

Master Photographers' Association (MPA)
1 West Ruislip Station, Ickenham Road, Ruislip, Middlesex HA4 7DW

Ministry of Defence (PE)
CMS 2, Empire Hotel, Bath

The National Council for the Training of Journalists
Carlton House, Hemnall Street, Epping, Essex CM16 4NL; 0378 72395

Newspaper Society (Training Department)
Whitefriars House, 6 Carmelite Street, London EC4Y 0BL

Photographic Training Centre
Fulham Studio, 101 Farm Lane, London SW6

Polytechnics Central Admissions System (PCAS)
PO Box 67, Cheltenham, Gloucestershire GL50 3AP

Professional Photographic Laboratories Association (PPLA)
1 West Ruislip Station, Ruislip, Middlesex HA4 7DW

Royal Photographic Society (RPS)
The Octagon, Milsom Street, Bath, Avon BA1 1DN; 0225 62841

Scottish Vocational Education Council (SCOTVEC)
38 Queen's Street, Glasgow G1 3DY

Society of Picture Researchers and Editors (SPREd)
BM 259, London WC1N 3XX

Universities Central Council on Admissions (UCCA)
PO Box 28, Cheltenham, Gloucestershire GL50 1HY

NB In all correspondence remember to include a stamped, self-addressed envelope for reply.

Journals Carrying Job Advertisements

British Journal of Photography. Published by Henry Greenwood and Company Limited, 28 Great James Street, London WC1N 3HL; 01-404 4202

Broadcast. Published by Arrowhead Publishers, Unit 3, Park Works, Kingsley, Bordon, Hampshire GU35 9LX; 04203 3066. Editorial; 01-439 9756

Guardian (Monday edition carries creative media and marketing job advertisements). Published by Guardian Newspapers Ltd, 119 Farringdon Road, London EC1R 2ER

The Journalist. Published by the National Union of Journalists, 314 Gray's Inn Road, London WC1; 01-278 7916

Professional Photographer. Maclaren Publications, PO Box 109, Maclaren House, Scarbrook Road, Croydon CR9 1QH

Times Higher Educational Supplement. Published by Times Newspapers Ltd, Priory House, St John's Lane, London EC1M 4BX; 01-253 3000

UK Press Gazette. 244–249 Temple Chambers, Temple Avenue, London EC4; 01-583 6463

See also photographic employment agencies.

Reference

The British Journal Directory of Photographic Education. Published by Henry Greenwood and Company Limited, 28 Great James Street, London WC1N 3HL. The most up-to-date and encyclopaedic directory of photographic courses currently available, compiled by Edward Martin, Department of Visual Communication, Trent Polytechnic, Nottingham.

A useful reference book for those setting up as photographers is *Running Your Own Photographic Business* by John Rose and Linda Hankin, published by Kogan Page.

Also Available from Kogan Page

Changing Your Job After 35: The Daily Telegraph Guide (6th edition), Godfrey Golzen and Philip Plumbley
Directory of Opportunities in Management Accountancy
Directory of Opportunities in New Technology
Directory of Opportunities in Sales and Marketing
How to Get on in Marketing, Advertising and Public Relations: A Career Development Guide, ed Norman Hart and Norman Waite
Getting There: Jobhunting for Women, Margaret Wallis
Great Answers to Tough Interview Questions: How to Get the Job You Want, Martin John Yate
How to Choose a Career, Vivien Donald
How to Get a Highly Paid Job in the City, Richard Roberts and Luke Johnson
How to Win at the Job Game: A Guide for Executives, Edward J Parsons
Making a Living as a Rock Musician, Kim Ludman
Moving On From Teaching: Career Development for Teachers, Caroline Elton
Offbeat Careers: 60 Ways to Avoid Becoming an Accountant, Vivien Donald
Working Abroad: The Daily Telegraph Guide to Working and Living Overseas (11th edition), Godfrey Golzen
Working for Yourself: The Daily Telegraph Guide to Self-Employment (9th edition), Godfrey Golzen
Working for Yourself in the Arts and Crafts, Sarah Hosking
Writing for a Living (2nd edition), Ian Linton

Running Your Own Antiques Business, Noël Riley and Godfrey Golzen
Running Your Own Boarding Kennels, Sheila Zabawa
Running Your Own Building Business, Kim Ludman
Running Your Own Catering Business, Ursula Garner and Judy Ridgway
Running Your Own Driving School, Nigel Stacey
Running Your Own Hairdressing Salon, Christine Harvey and Helen Steadman
Running Your Own Mail Order Business, Malcolm Breckman
Running Your Own Photographic Business, John Rose and Linda Hankin
Running Your Own Pub, Elven Money
Running Your Own Restaurant, Diane Hughes and Godfrey Golzen
Running Your Own Shop, Roger Cox
Running Your Own Small Hotel, Joy Lennick
Running Your Own Typing Service, Doreen Huntley
Running Your Own Wine Bar, Judy Ridgway